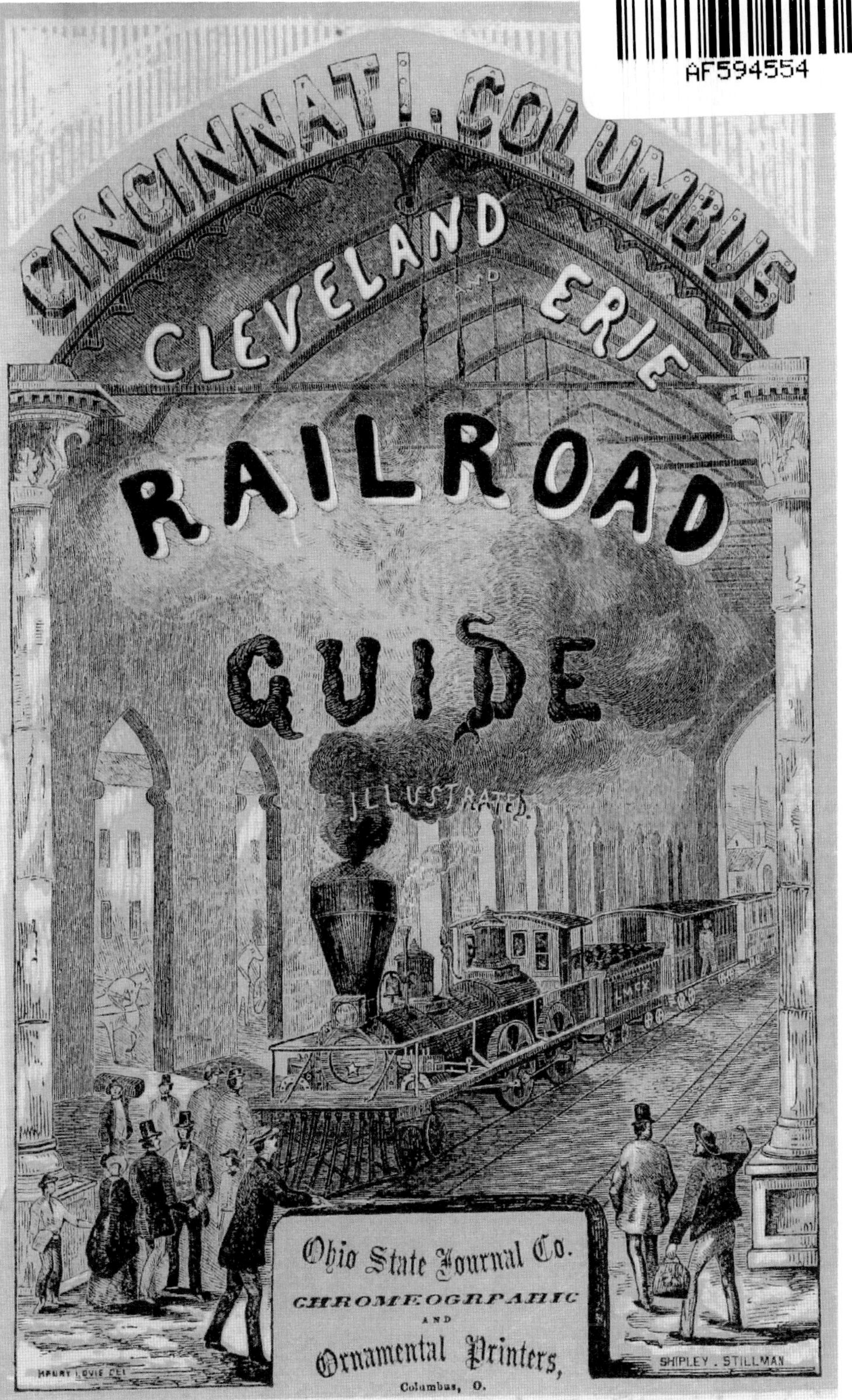
CINCINNATI. COLUMBUS
CLEVELAND AND ERIE
RAILROAD
GUIDE
ILLUSTRATED.
Ohio State Journal Co.
CHROMEOGRPAHIC
AND
Ornamental Printers,
Columbus, O.
SHIPLEY . STILLMAN

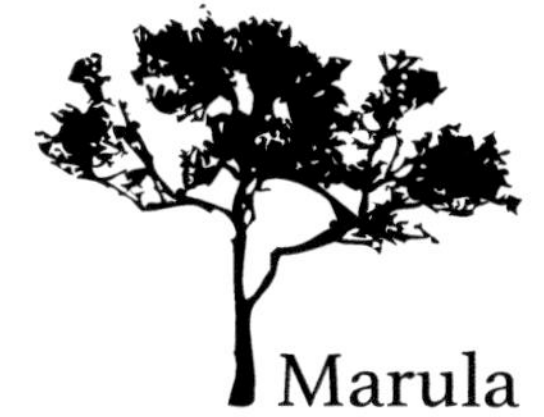

An imprint of Arcadia Publishing

The Ohio Railroad Guide
Cincinnati to Erie, via Columbus and Cleveland
Ohio State Journal Company

A Marula Historical Reprint
Originally published in 1854

Published by Arcadia Publishing
Charleston SC

ISBN 978-0-7385-9473-6

Printed in the United States of America

For all general information contact Arcadia Publishing at:
Telephone 843-853-2070
Fax 843-853-0044
E-mail sales@arcadiapublishing.com
For customer service and orders:
Toll-Free 1-888-313-2665

Visit us on the Internet at www.arcadiapublishing.com

THE

OHIO RAILROAD GUIDE,

ILLUSTRATED.

CINCINNATI TO ERIE,

VIA

COLUMBUS AND CLEVELAND.

COLUMBUS:
OHIO STATE JOURNAL COMPANY.
1854.

LIST OF ILLUSTRATIONS.

THE ILLUSTRATED GUIDE.

TRAVELER!——whoever thou art——stop one moment, to contemplate the progress and grandeur of this Western Empire! In Europe, Asia and Africa, you will be called to admire ancient castles, ruined temples, fallen columns, and all the evidences of a magnificence which is either already old, or fallen to decay. It was achieved by labor—put forth in ages past—and is made interesting and glorious, by memories and associations which are now only historical. The banks of the Rhine, still populous with its millions, are thus filled with the castellated remains of former greatness. The Nile, the Tigris and the Euphrates, are lined with the ruins of Thebes and Heliopolis, of Babylon, of Nineveh, and those thousands of cities and temples, which once stood glorious monuments of ancient magnificence—the pride and admiration of a world! *There* you stand amidst ruins. All is absorbed in memory! All testifies to the mutation of human affairs—to Decline and Fall.

Now look around you! — Mark what you see! — You have passed to the very antipodes of scene, and time, and event. The Past is gone; the Present lives before you. The new Empire is not falling, but rising to glory and grandeur. There rolls the Ohio, graceful in its curves, surrounded with green hills, but crowned with no castles,— having no memories save those of the red Indian, who disappeared but yesterday, and calling up no association of Egyptian or Gothic gods — of Cambyses, Frederick, or Napoleon, leading the heavy tramp of armies, in the career of war and conquest. Some border wars of the early time there have been, but none which destroyed or revolutionized nations. The white man came to possess a land which none had cultivated, and here, all around you, are the peaceful fruits of his labors. The thronged city, with its work-shops, its marts, its stores, its canals, its roads, its churches and schools; the vine-clad hills, the Corinthian house, the distant cottage, the observatory of science — and all that the labor and art of the modern can furnish — are here, on the banks of the Beautiful River. Whence came this magic creation? Is it due to the sacrifice of blood? to the conquests of a great hero? to the government of an illustrious monarch? to the well-ordered discipline of feudal retainers? — Or to some extraordinary performance of human genius? or to some miraculous interposition of Providence?

To none of these is this creation due, though this land has received the richest gifts of Nature, and the smiles of Providence. It is, however, the work of an ancient knight — one who dwelt in Egypt, Greece, and Rome, in their golden times, but has now left their ruins gray, to inhabit and invigorate this new and rising Empire. The Knight of Industry is his name, and he it is who has cultured the fields; and

> "The towns has quicken'd by mechanic arts,
> And bade the fervent city glow with toil."

In truth, all that you see in this metropolis of the Ohio Valley, is the result of only half a century of *hard work*. This is a plain term, but it expresses the whole. Only a little more than half a century since, the red Indian contended for the site of Cincinnati, and the stockade — Fort Washington — was the only strong-hold of the white in this valley. Soon the Indian disappeared; the hut became useless, and was abandoned; the town grew up, at first only a dirty village, and now a great and prosperous city, full of art, commerce, and wealth. No where else can so entire a transformation, accomplished in so short a time, be found. Viewed in its just light, it is a far greater wonder than any of the old and renowned ruins of the earth. It is not wonderful, that Time and Decay should destroy the mightiest work of man, or that man should be capable of great works, when he has time sufficient; but that he should perform the work of centuries in a single generation, and that he should transform the dark wilderness into the fruitful field and blooming garden, within the limits of a life, seems like the marvels of an Oriental story, or rather like the fulfillment of those ancient prophecies, which speak of the desert blooming like the rose. But — the cars are starting — let us note what we see on the way.

The LITTLE MIAMI RAIL ROAD did not exist twelve years since — nor any other railway in the Valley of the Ohio — but now it is here, to take you on your journey with all the speed, comfort and convenience of any such road, in any country; and there are three thousand miles of railway in this valley! Year after year hundreds of miles are added to the number, and where it once took weeks to accomplish a journey, it now takes only hours! What a revolution! But the revolution is not in the gain of time only, nor even money. The great change is in society. Thousands meet now where tens could meet twenty years since. Look through these cars, and you see around, men, women and children going to see friends, or transact business, or seeking pleasure, where they would not have dreamed of going a few years since. Some are going only to the next town; some to the Lakes; some to the Atlantic; some to Europe; — and some, perhaps, will wander through old Jerusalem, or by the banks of Jordan, before they

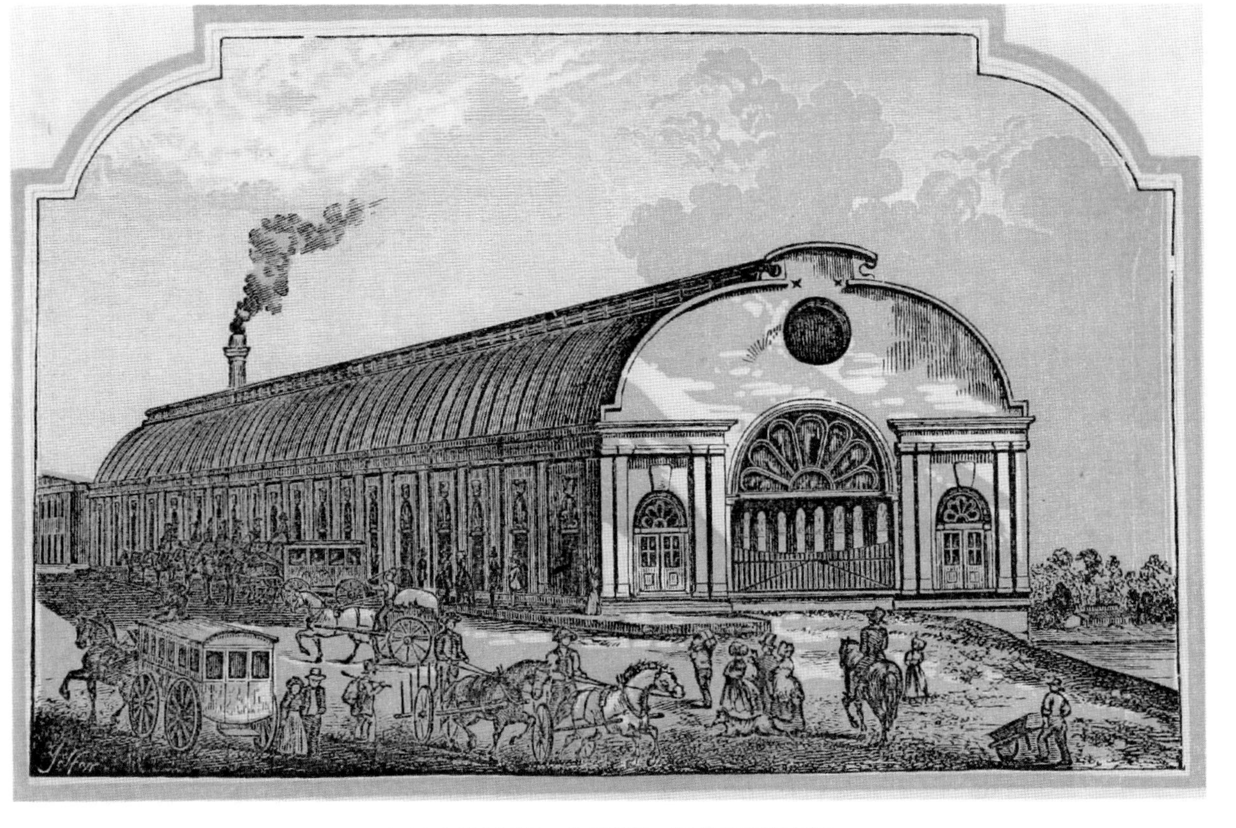

PASSENGER DEPOT, CINCINNATI.

will again return. The Railroad and the Steamboat have made man almost ubiquitous on this little earth, and his fondness for novelty and change is gratified beyond the dreams of fancy. Where will this stop? No where, till this earth is inhabited by one family, dwelling together in peace and unity.

Before we start, let us look at this DEPOT. I have seen many fine depots, in the east and the west — some of solid, beautiful stone — but I have seen none more spacious or convenient than this. It is recently finished; and there will be need of all its accommodations, for the immense congregation of persons and things, gathering here from the numerous lines of railway, North and East. Already there are five or six hundred miles of Ohio Railroads, whose whole business with Cincinnati centres here, and the number is continually increasing. This building is 465 feet long, 90 feet wide, and 30 feet high. It is, as you see, built in the most solid manner, and beautifully arched. It covers just an acre of ground, and would contain ten thousand people. On the opposite side you will see another Depot, also very large. In these depots, and in the machine shop beyond, are included four or five acres of ground, nearly covered with buildings, and all absolutely necessary to accommodate the immense business of the Railway.

Before we start, let us recognize the *localities*

around the Depot. We are now just at the foot of DEER CREEK, over which is the stone bridge you have just passed. This little stream is only two miles in length, originating on the top of the northern hills, and running down the ravine in which you see the MIAMI CANAL, whose outlet is just below the bridge. The creek is now covered most of the way by a stone culvert. At the head of it, about a mile above the Depot, are the principal slaughtering establishments; and in former years, I have seen the creek running with blood, from the hogs killed upon it. In the cold weather of December and January, thousands of these animals are slaughtered each day, and the stream is crimsoned till it mingles with the Ohio.

Up Deer Creek ravine, if you cast a look, factories, foundries and mills arise in continual succession far as the eye can see. Most of them are turned by the water power of the canal; but some are carried on by steam, which is now very cheap. This is one of the busiest parts of the town, and an immensely heavy business is transacted in its neighborhood. Sugar mills for Louisiana, locomotives for railways, machinery of all kinds, linseed oil, flour, candles, soap, and numerous other articles, are manufactured in Deer Creek valley. The value of these manufactures, in this little ravine alone, amounts to some three or four millions of dollars per annum; and yet it is but a small part of what is done in Cincinnati.

Now let us glance at something very different. Out of sight, but on the summit of the hill just to your left, is the OBSERVATORY. The hill on which it stands is called MOUNT ADAMS, from John Quincy Adams, who laid the corner-stone of the building. The Observatory was founded by Professor Mitchell, whose untiring exertions procured subscriptions among all classes of people, which, with his own labor and perseverance, accomplished the work. The structure is quite a handsome one, and fitted with the larger class of astronomical instruments, though it still needs many of the minor appurtenances of a complete one. The great equatorial Telescope is one of the finest in the world, and is to the eye, as well as to science, really magnificent. The focal length is 17½ feet, and the diameter of the object glass 12 inches. It is mounted on a stone pedestal of great strength, and is made of the most beautiful brass, polished to the brightness of a mirror. Although weighing 2,500 pounds, it may be moved to any point with your little finger, so nicely adjusted are the pivots and wheels on which it moves. Should the stranger in Cincinnati ever find an opportunity, he will be delighted with the scenery of the siderial heavens, presented through this glass. Saturn, with its golden rings; the Moon, and her dim and shadowy mountains; Jupiter, and his attendant satelites

— all are beautiful and lovely, and, to one who has never seen this telescopic vision, most wonderful.

It is very singular, yet true, that this same hill was once used as an Indian observatory; but not to observe the heavens—nor look through telescopes—nor count the glowing orbs, as they career through the skies. No; the Indian made an observatory of the tops of the high trees on the hill, to see what the white men were doing in the fort below. A lady, whose husband was an officer in Fort Washington, told me that White Eyes, an Indian chief, said that he had often climbed to the top of the "big tree" on the hill, and looked down into Fort Washington, where he could see every movement. This was just before Wayne's victory in 1795. That gave peace to the valley, and border wars were known no more. One short generation has passed, and what marvels are seen! Yonder little stream, then filled with alder bushes, and musical with birds, is now crowded with lofty factories, and thundering with the din of machinery and the roar of wheels. Where the old fort was, rises lofty domes, and towers, and turrets, surrounded with the gay splendor of a modern city. On yonder hill — then forest-crowned — rises the Observatory; and the red Indian,

"Whose soul proud science never taught to stray
Far as the solar walk or milky way,"

is replaced by the bold white, who seeks to penetrate the depths of the sky, and reveal the mysteries of heaven!

—Hark! the bell rings, and we shall soon leave Cincinnati behind us. The first object which strikes the eye on the right, is the large building of the CINCINNATI WATER WORKS, usually pouring forth a dark cloud of coal smoke. Being carried on by steam, these works have none of the beauty of Fairmount (Philadelphia), so justly celebrated. They are, nevertheless, interesting from the great scale on which they are constructed, and the immense work they perform. Cincinnati is built on a great plain, with two levels, or steps; one of which is 55 feet, and the other 108 feet above low water mark. Hence to supply it with water from the river, this water must first be raised 150 feet above its lowest stage, in order to acquire head enough to cause a flow through all the pipes. Now, when we consider that nearly two hundred thousand people are to be supplied with water from this source, it may be imagined that the power required is immense. This work is done by iron forcing pumps, moved by steam. The barrel of the main pump is 18 inches diameter, and 8 feet stroke of piston. There are two pumps which can throw five millions of gallons each twelve hours. The daily consumption of the city is about 2,500,000 gallons. By these pumps the water is forced into a reservoir, on the hill above, and thence carried in pipes to all parts of the city. This reservoir is 368 feet long, 135 feet wide, and 23 feet deep, capable of containing one million cubic gallons of water. The containing walls are of stone, several feet in thickness, double, with an interval between, and thoroughly cemented. From this reservoir, the water is carried to all parts of the city in iron pipes, of which the main stem is 20 inches in diameter. The pipes now make about sixty miles in length, and supply 15,000 hydrants.

Just beyond us, on the right, is another long, dingy volcanic establishment, pouring forth flame and smoke. This is the Rolling Mill of Shreve, Steele & Co., and may be taken as a sample of the numerous iron factories in Cincinnati. The part of the city where we now are is almost wholly occupied with mills, factories, and machine shops of various kinds; and the dwellings are of a cheap structure, occupied chiefly by work people. Hence there is little beauty in it, and, like the first view of most cities seen from public conveyances, does not strike a stranger as very imposing. The same characteristic appearance prevails for five miles, in which there is a continuous street passing through towns of different names, but in fact only prolongations of Cincinnati. Next to the city, in succession, are FULTON, PENDLETON, SPENCER, and COLUMBIA. Nothing, however, indicates where either begin, or end. They are only suburbs. As we pass along, there will be seen — notwithstanding the dingy look of houses and shops — some beautiful, as well as interesting things. By keeping your attention mainly fixed on the right, or river side of the cars, you will see the Kentucky hills in some of their most graceful attitudes. The forest is not half cleared off, but near the river there are green fields, country seats, and villages; forming, altogether, quite a picturesque landscape. The hills have the contour and height which characterize nearly the whole thousand miles of the Ohio Valley. Above Wheeling they are more abrupt, and below the Cumberland less in height; but what you see before you is the general character of the hills which bound the Ohio, and which, with its winding curves, have given it the name of the "Beautiful River." They are gentle in their ascent, without rock or precipice, gracefully curved on every side, and covered with rich and abundant foliage. All bear the aspect of beauty and gentleness. There is nothing of the sublime, the abrupt, or the rough. Hence he who compares the scenery of the Ohio with that of the Hudson, or the St. Lawrence, does injustice to both. They are not alike. There are no such sublime heights as those of the Highlands, nor such island-covered breadth of waters as on the St. Lawrence; but neither have they anything like the graceful windings, the gentle hills, the broad bottoms, the deep green of foliage, which gives such loveliness to the vale of the Ohio. Just above this, is a most picturesque curve, with the winding town on this side, the green hills of Kentucky on the other, the river bending away around the base of the hills till lost to the sight, and curling smoke rising in fleecy clouds to the sky. Beyond that, and about six miles from Cincinnati (almost all of which is the village), on the Ohio side, is the Little Miami, from which our Road takes its name.

I have been descending the river in one of the fine Pittsburgh packets, in the beginning of May. Deep was the foliage of the forest, velvet-like the soft green of the fields; rapid and rolling the river, the wind raising on its surface the little "white tops," and bringing with it the balmy freshness of the woods. Then the Ohio is indeed beautiful; then I could say, with truth —

"See the rivers how they run,
Through woods and meads, in shade and sun,
Sometimes swift, sometimes slow,
Wave succeeding wave, they go
A various journey to the deep."

The name OHIO was given originally by the Indians, and signified nearly the same, as the French termed it, "La belle Riviere;" but conveying the idea of white water, or white waves.

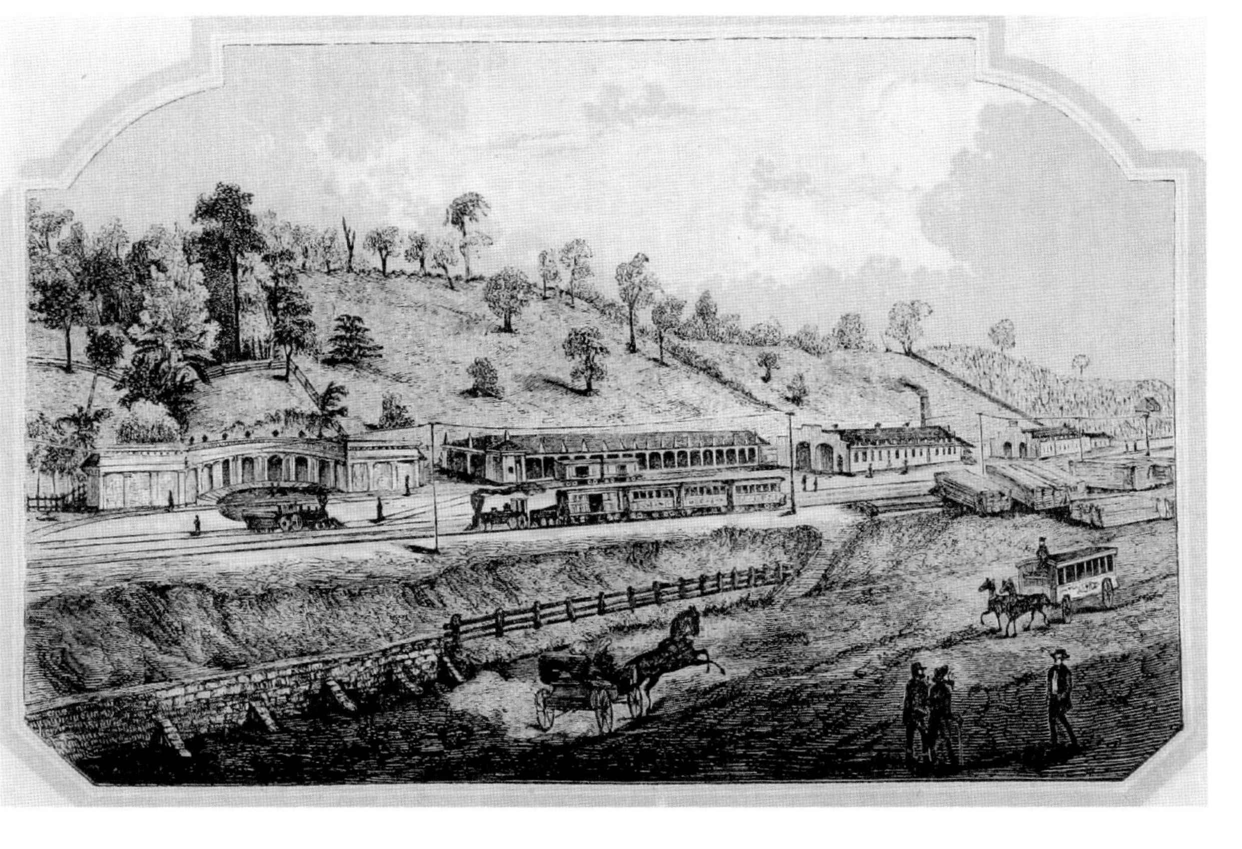

CAR SHOPS AND ENGINE DEPOT, PENDLETON, L. M. R. R.

On the right, and near two miles from the Depot, you will see a handsome town on the Kentucky shore. This is JAMESTOWN. It was laid out only three or four years since, and is now, as you see, a considerable village. In a few years, the Kentucky shore, like the Ohio, will be lined with a continuous town. The three towns of Covington, Newport and Jamestown, now contain about twenty thousand inhabitants. Three-fourths of this is the growth of the last ten years.

PENDLETON is three miles from Cincinnati, but is only a continuance of the town we have passed. The Company have here a large stable for locomotives, a machine shop, repair shop, work-shops, &c., &c. The accompanying plate gives a view of this establishment.

The cars were formerly compelled to move slow from the depot to this point; but the Company having purchased the ground, at immense expense, for their own use, there is now no interruption, and we move swiftly on.

From Pendleton we pass rapidly into the Valley of the Miami. Almost imperceptibly, the cars turn more than a quarter circle; leaving a high hill, on the left, the summit of which is called TUSCULUM, and occupied as a peach orchard and vineyard. From this hill is one of the finest views in America,—commanding the suburbs of Cincinnati, the Valley of the Little Miami, and the beautiful curves and surroundings of the Ohio. It is well worth while for a traveler in Ohio, to drive, some clear morning (as he may, on a good road), to take a view of this charming scene. If, when we gaze with delight from yonder hill, the red Indian could return, he might well exclaim, with Roderick Dhu,—

> "Saxon, from yonder mountain high,
> I marked thee send delighted eye,
> Far to the south and east, where lay
> Extended, in succession gay,
> Deep waving fields and pastures green,
> With gentle slopes and groves between.
> These fertile plains, that spotted vale,
> Were once the birthright of the Gael;
> The stranger came, with iron hand,
> And from our fathers reft the land.
> Where dwell we now?"——

It is in vain; neither Roderick nor the Indian can regain their native land. And why should they? The earth must be cultivated; and it is not the wild hunter nor the Highland robber can do that. Civilization must prevail, and sympathy is wasted upon those who, either for want of will or capacity, or Providential favor, are unable to perform their part in reducing the wilderness to cultivation, and the human mind to discipline. This work of cultivation and discipline is what we see before us. This Railway is one of the highest types of Physical Progress, and the science by which it is accomplished, one of the highest evidences of intellectual discipline.

Now look to the right, as you turn, and take a view of the broad fields of the Miami Valley. The river runs on the other side, in a narrow grove of trees, which conceals it from your sight, and joins the Ohio about a mile and a half from the turn round the hill. Few spots present a richer view of the fertile soil of Ohio, in its products, than this vale in mid-summer, when the Indian corn waves its tassels, the meadows are verdant, and here and there a market garden has a little patch blooming with various plants.

The FIRST BURYING GROUND is six miles from Cincinnati, near where we are. It is just to the right, a narrow inclosure, with a few old tombs yet visible. It is the burial place of the first settlers,—for COLUMBIA was settled before Cincinnati. The first colony was composed of Mr. Stites and twenty-six others, who landed here in 1788. The failure of this settlement was owing to the fact of these bottoms being overflowed at high water, so that, in the very next year, all the cabins but one were under water. Oliver Spencer, one of the earliest inhabitants of Cincinnati, says of Columbia: "Fresh in my remembrance is the rude log house, the first humble sanctuary of the first settlers of Columbia, standing amidst the tall forest trees, on the beautiful knoll where now is a grave-yard, and the ruins of a Baptist meeting house of later years. There, on the holy Sabbath, we were wont to assemble to hear the word of life; but our fathers met with their muskets and rifles, prepared for action, and ready to repel any attack of the enemy. And while the watchman on the walls of Zion was uttering his faithful and pathetic warning, the sentinels without, at a few rods' distance, with measured step, were now pacing their walks, and, with strained eyes, endeavoring to pierce through the distance, carefully scanning every object that seemed to have life or motion."

The first clergyman who preached in the old log church was Mr. GANO, the father of General Gano, one of the early settlers. Daniel Gano, for many years Clerk of the Courts in Cincinnati, was born here—one of the oldest living men born on the soil of Ohio.

In this little, unpretending grave-yard, were buried the early dead of Ohio. They went to sleep in the wilderness, but their bones lie amidst hundreds of thousands, who now live where the wilderness stood. Of them may truly be said,—

> Beneath those rugged elms, that locust's shade,
>   Where heaves the turf in many a mouldering heap,
> Each in his narrow cell forever laid,
>   The rude forefathers of the hamlet sleep.

They were not so *very* rude; for most of the settlers

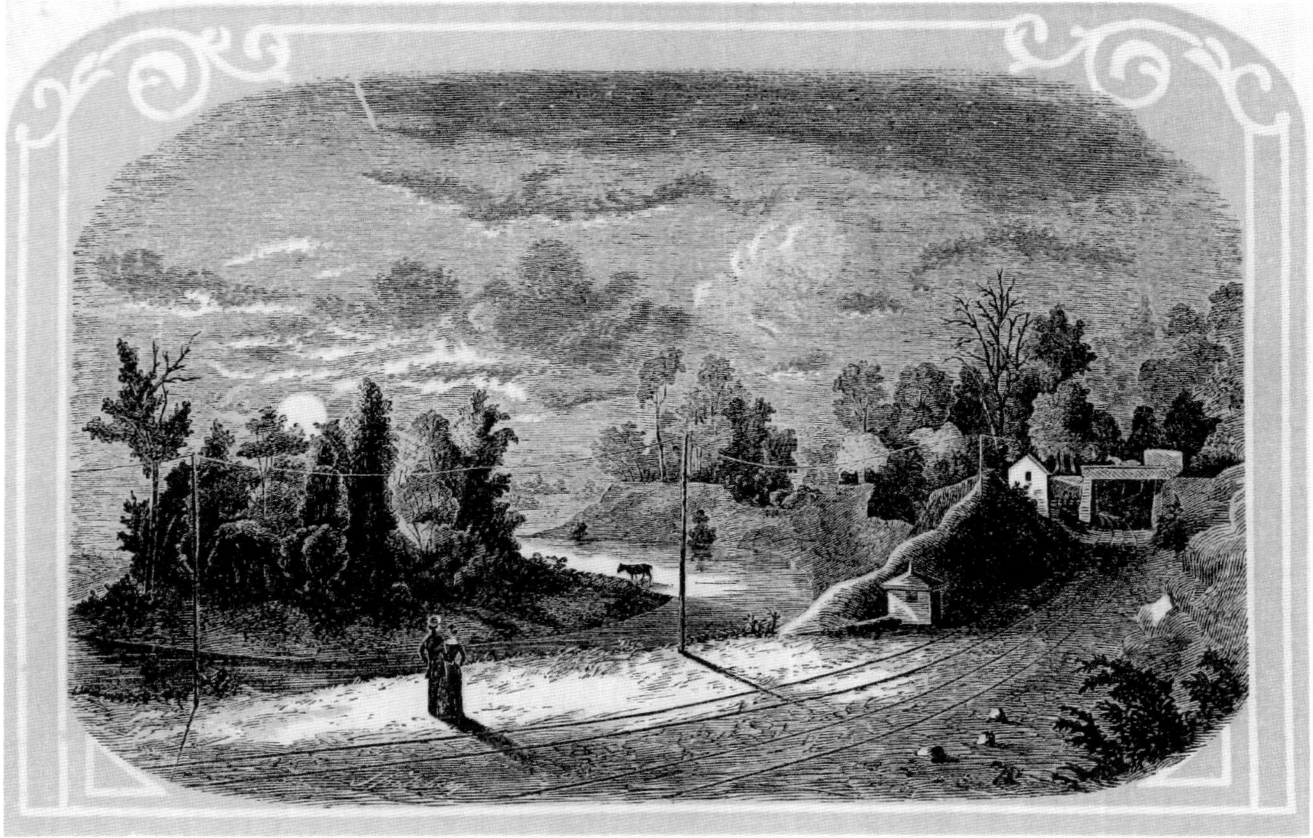

SCENE BY MOONLIGHT AT RED BANK.

of Ohio, were intelligent men. But these were the *forefathers*—and not of a *hamlet* only; nor merely of a common city; but doubtless of some modern Babylon or London, which here rising on the banks of the Ohio, shall rival the renowned cities of the earth.

The cars are flying on, and we hasten too. We are now passing over a little stream called DUCK CREEK, and truly it is a very good *duck* creek, and there is some pleasant shade along its banks. We now come on to the MIAMI RIVER, which you will see on one side or the other, for more than fifty miles. I may as well introduce you now to the character and history of the Miami, whose company you are to keep for so long a time. This river rises in the western edge of Madison county; thence traverses a part of Clarke; and thence through Greene, Warren, and part of Clermont and Hamilton. Its whole length is about 80 miles, and its descent in that distance, about 700 feet; or, an average of about 9 feet to a mile. This rapid, but generally equable descent, makes it an admirable mill stream —and there are in the valley of the Miami, numerous mills and factories, most of whose products go to Cincinnati. There are a million and two hundred thousand bushels of wheat, grown in this valley; and at least four millions of bushels of corn. These, of course, cause a large export of flour, hogs and whisky, which furnish heavy freights for the Little

Miami Railroad, and bring a most profitable tribute to Cincinnati. Notwithstanding the fall in the river is so great, the current is gentle,—and the whole scenery is soft. Generally, the trees and shrubs on the banks, are suffered to grow—and the river is seen through the foliage. We pursue the valley very closely, till we reach Xenia, where we leave it, and bend over the upland plain towards Columbus.

The Little Miami is one of two streams with the same name—the other being nearly parallel—at about twenty miles distance. From these streams, this district is called the MIAMI VALLEY, and is celebrated for its fertility. The whole section, watered by the two Miamis, contains seven thousand square miles, and more than half a million of inhabitants. This gives seventy to the square mile, and a density of habitation, equal to New England, except in the immediate vicinity of Boston.

The Miami Valley was first noticed by Washington, who having crossed the Alleghenies himself one hundred years ago, seems to have been well informed upon the character of the country and climate, on the Ohio. In a letter to a friend, written after the revolution, he mentions the country on the Miamis—as described to him by surveyors, who had visited it—as remarkably fine in soil and climate. It is singular also, that Washington should also be the first person to project the formation of the present State of Ohio. I never saw this mentioned in any history or discussion of the subject; but so it is. In a letter to a gentleman of New York, he recommends the purchase of the Indian lands, rather than a war with them. For, he says, their lands are all you can get by war—and you can get them by purchase. With that remarkable sagacity for which Washington was so distinguished, he says the purchase of the lands and settlement by the whites, go together. Hence, he recommends that a State be formed on the north side of the Ohio—whose western boundary should run through the mouth of the Great Miami, and be continued to the Miami of the Lakes, and thence to Lake Erie. The State would be comprehended between this western boundary and Pennsylvania, and between Lake Erie and the Ohio River. This is precisely the present State of Ohio, and within twenty years from the writing of Washington's letter, it was admitted into the Union. I mention this little episode, to illustrate the practical sense and foresight of him, who in fact, not less than in name, was the Father of his Country.

As we pass along, and the variegated foliage of trees and shrubs and plants appears before us, it may interest us a little to know what they are. We are not botanists or florists; but the common plants of each district of country should be noted by every observing traveler. The Oak and the Sugar Maple, we find in almost every part of our wide country. But there are numerous plants, which are peculiar to certain districts, and often to very small districts. This peculiarity seems, to depend (setting aside climate) on some peculiarity in the soil, or structure of the earth's surface—what the Geologists call its *formation*—or, as I should say, its composition. I know little about Geology; but one leading fact I can tell you. This Miami country is all of it a *limestone* country. The farmers say that lime is one great cause of the fertility of the soil. At any rate, this lime certainly encourages the growth of some plants, and is hostile to others. Now, let us see what plants we have before us. It is spring, and we see Nature and her children to advantage. If not in their most valuable, they are certainly in their most beautiful dresses. I shall not enumerate the common trees, but merely mention some that are the most characteristic of this region. In early spring, may be seen the REDBUD (*Cercis*), which bears a beautiful red bud, and seems like a jewel on the breast of the forest. Flowering about the same time, is the Dogwood (*Cornus*), which bears a large white flower, shaded with a little yellow. The Flowering LOCUST (*Robinia*), comes later, and when in blossom is a beautiful tree. The BUCKEYE (*Æsculus maxima*), has given name to the inhabitants of Ohio. The POISON VINE, (*Rhus Radicans*) is a very common plant in summer, and by

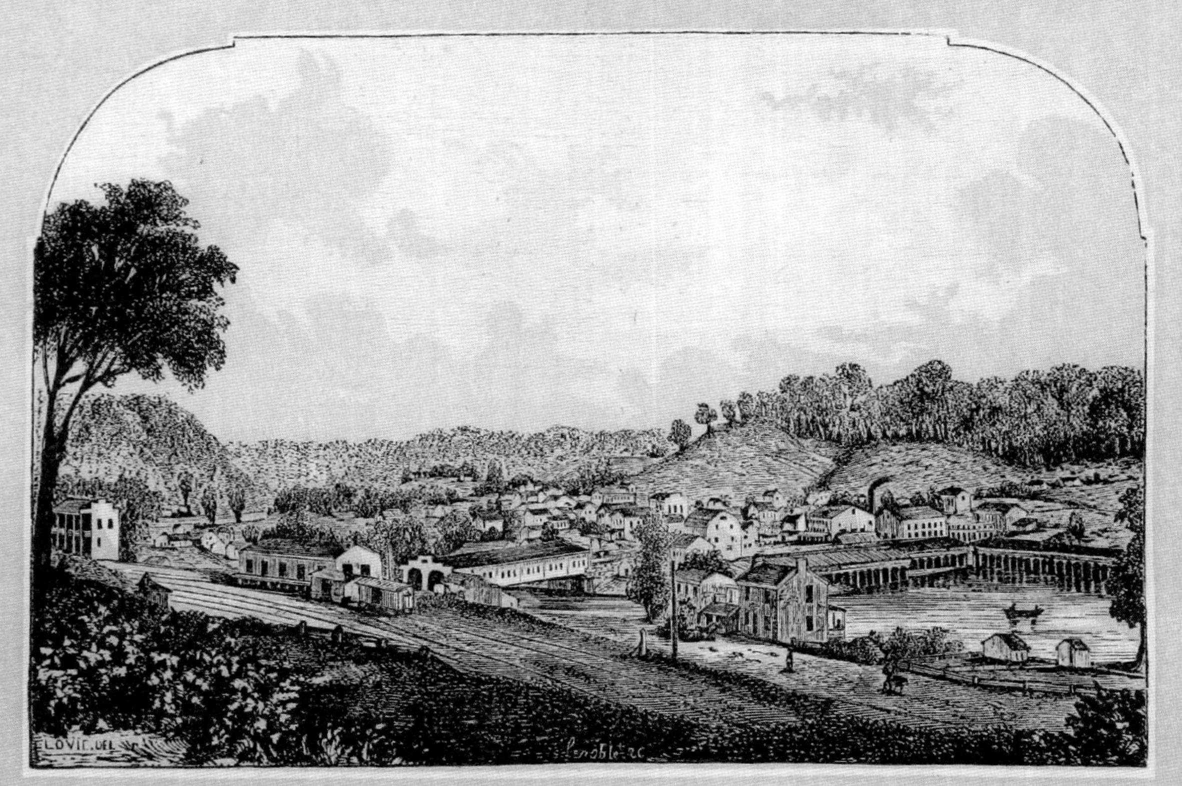

VIEW OF MILFORD.

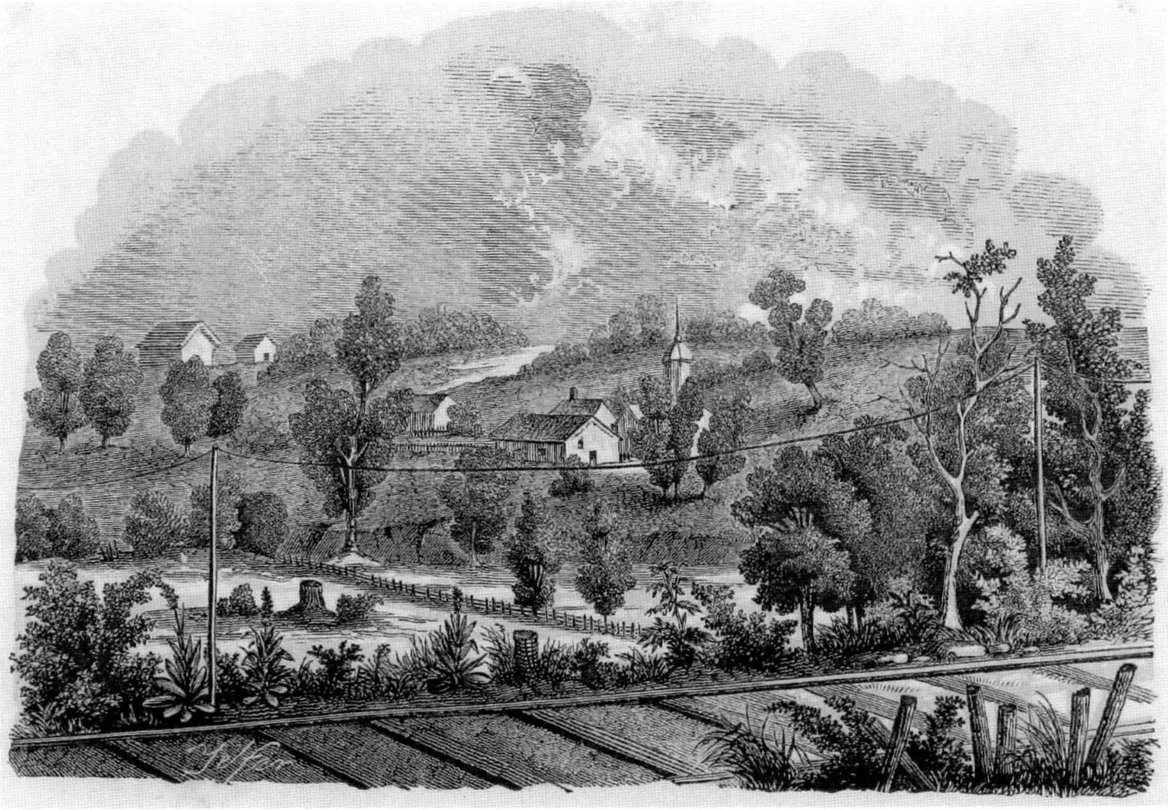

VIEW NEAR MILFORD.

many, is supposed to be the cause of milk sickness, which was a very afflicting disease in some sections of the country below Columbus; but in the progress of cultivation, seems to have nearly disappeared. The INDIAN ARROW WOOD, (*Euonymus*) is abundant in mid-summer. The PAWPAW (*Anona Glebra*), is very common in the neighborhood of all our streams, and with the Buckeye boy, its fruit is quite a favorite. The TULIP TREE (*poplar*), in its season, bears a very fine flower. The WILD CHERRY, CRAB APPLE, PERSIMMON, HONEY LOCUST, WILD PLUM, the ASPEN and the BOX, are common trees of the country. The most numerous timber trees, are the Sugar Maple, Beech, White Oak, Walnut, Ash and Hickory.

The Miami country has no Pine; nor is there any district of pine trees within several hundred miles. Hence the transportation of pine lumber to Cincinnati—where it is so much needed—is an extensive business. In the future, pine boards will probably be brought by railway, from the distant regions of Michigan, Wisconsin and Minnesota.

PLAINVILLE, to the left, is a station 9½ miles from Cincinnati, and 6½ from Pendleton Engine Shops. There is nothing peculiar about it,—though the situation is pleasant; and a number of gentlemen have purchased the neighboring heights for rural residences.

The Miami, here and below, affords several mill seats, which have been occupied for many years. In the first settlement of the country, they used a very different kind of mill. A little grinding apparatus was fixed in a boat, and the boat being anchored, the wheel at the side was turned by the current. Others of the pioneers—especially in Kentucky—used horse mills and hand mills. Thus, the first settlement of the West approached very nearly the primitive state,—when the simplest arts and usages were adopted.

MILFORD, on the right, is 14 miles from Cincinnati, and is a very interesting place. It is in Clermont county, (we are now in Hamilton) and on the other side of the Miami. The village contains probably 600 inhabitants. The spires of its churches and schools, are conspicuous in the scene. The great mill, and long row of sheds to the right, are Kugler's Mills and Distillery: the sheds are for hogs, which are fed from the refuse of the distillery. Just in front, is the bridge which connects the Depot with Milford, and over which passes a turnpike road to the country beyond. There are three or four stages and omnibuses waiting here to convey passengers to the interior. The county of Clermont is fertile and populous—furnishing a large business to the Railway and Cincinnati.

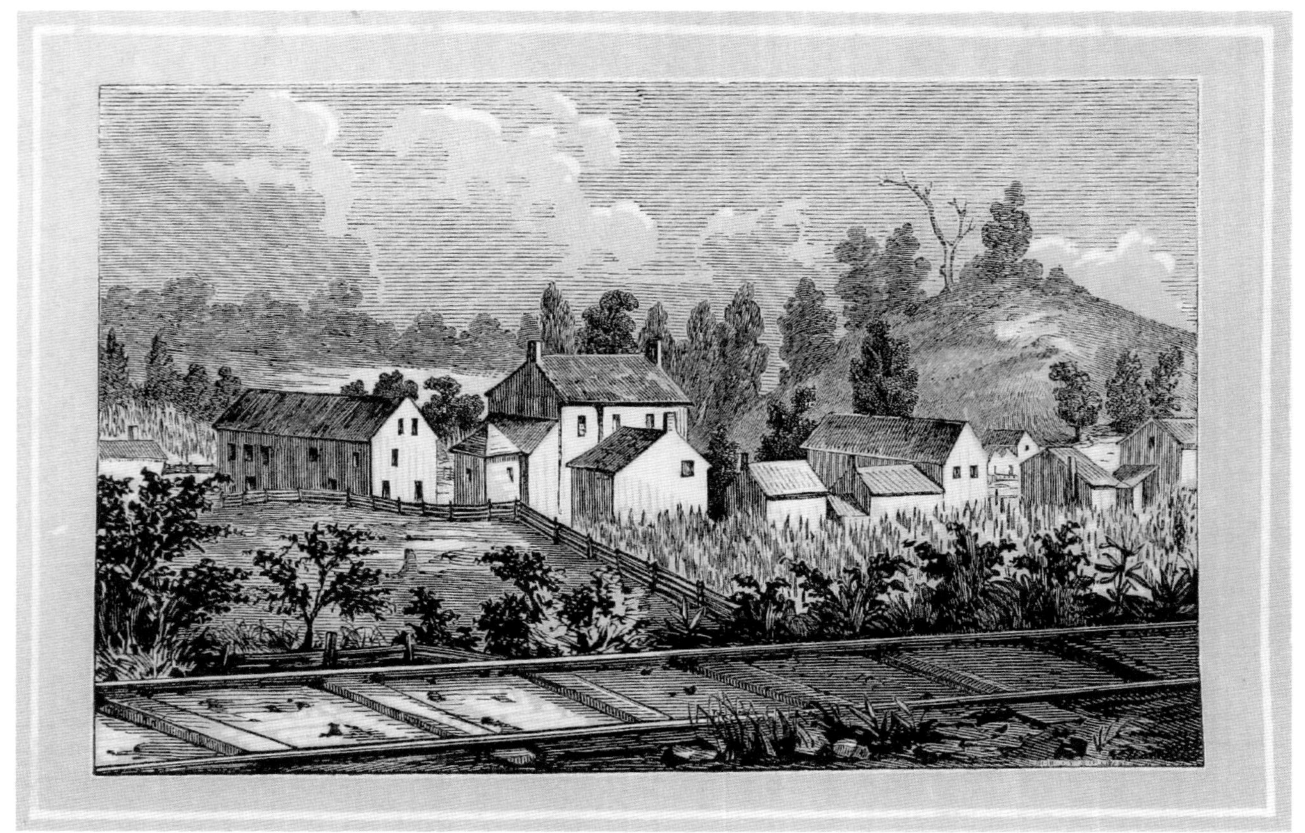

VIEW OF GERMANY

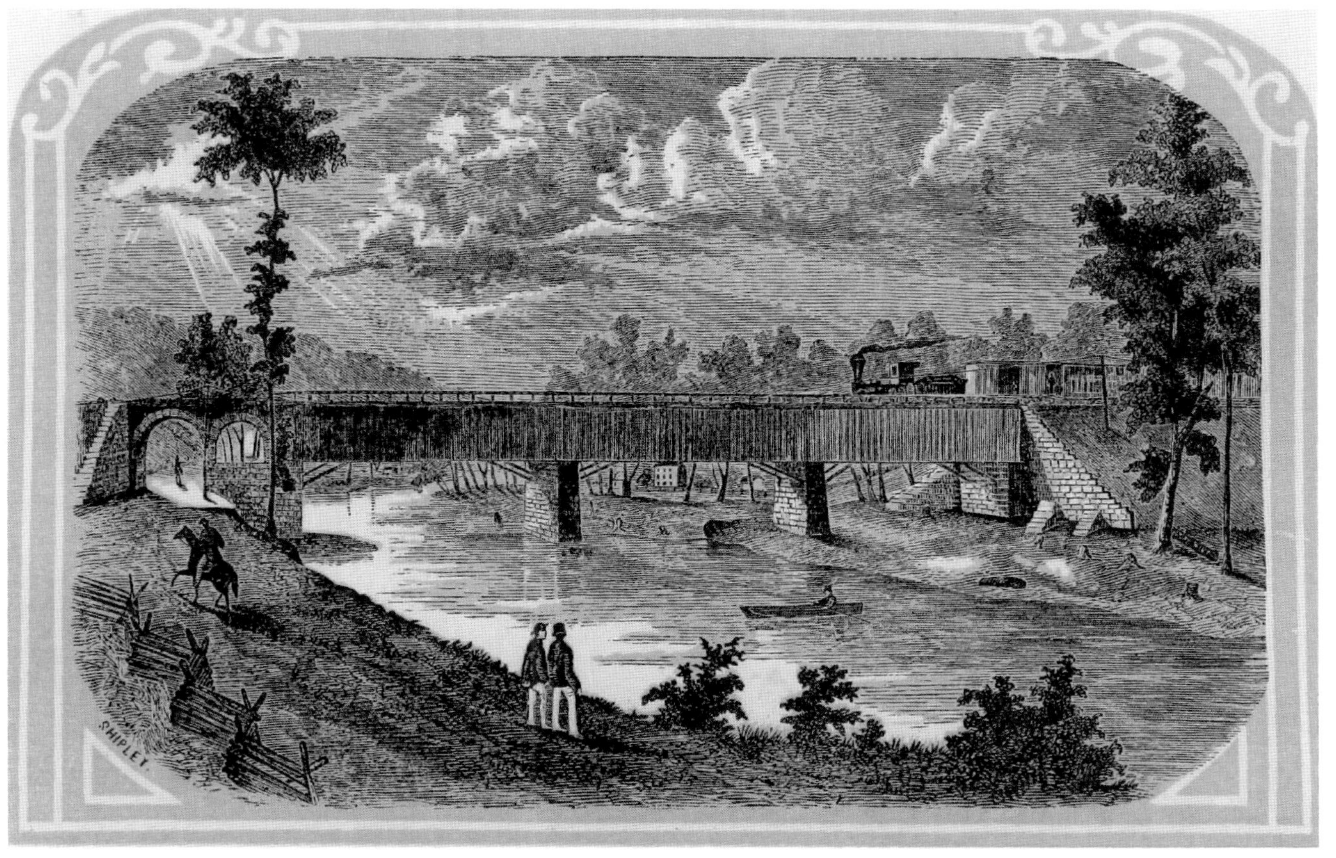

BRIDGE OVER LITTLE MIAMI AT MIAMIVILLE.

Just beyond — as the cars pass — there is a dam over the Miami, which furnishes a very pretty waterfall. This dam supplies the water power to the mills below.

The plate, page 21, represents a rural scene just above Milford — and is characteristic of the country. The gentle swell of hills, the quiet repose of farm houses, and the intermingling of native woods with cultivation, are the principal features of Ohio scenery in this part of the State. The sublime and rugged are not here; but the gentle and graceful predominate.

GERMANY, about 16 miles from Cincinnati, is a little villa. The scene in the plate represents the residence of M. Kugler, Esq., proprietor of the large Mill and Distillery seen at Milford.

MIAMI BRIDGE is about 18 miles from Cincinnati. Here the Railroad passes to the east side of the Miami, and continues on that side for fifty miles. The bridge is a substantial structure,— constructed for a double track — and above high water. A view is given in the accompanying plate.

MIAMIVILLE is a little village on the left, grown up by the location of mills, and the construction of the Railway.

LOVELAND, 23 miles from Cincinnati, is an important station. Here is the intersection of the Hillsborough Railroad with the Little Miami Railroad.

Hillsborough is 37 miles by rail, from this point. It is the county seat of Highland county, and a pleasant village. It is situated on a hill, 1074 feet above tide-water, and 600 feet above Cincinnati. This hill, and the surrounding ridges, however, are all of gentle curvature, so as to seem nothing but a rolling country—variegated with forest and field. Thus situated, it is very healthy—and in summer a cool and agreeable retreat. The village contains about 2,000 inhabitants, with several churches. The society is cultivated and agreeable.

The Hillsborough Railroad, is, as yet, only constructed from Loveland to Hillsborough, 37 miles; but is in course of construction to Jackson, and may be continued to Parkersburg. Such was the original intention; but the Company has recently been united with the Cincinnati and Marietta Company, which goes to the same point. At Parkersburg, it will be connected with the Baltimore railways, making a continuous Baltimore line to Cincinnati.

At LOVELAND, the Miami and Hillsborough lines unite; the whole distance from Hillsborough to Cincinnati being 60 miles. Three or four years since, there was but a single house here; but now, there is quite a village grown up. The junction of the Railways is seen in the opposite plate.

FOSTER'S CROSSINGS is on the left, and takes its name from the original resident here. It is simply

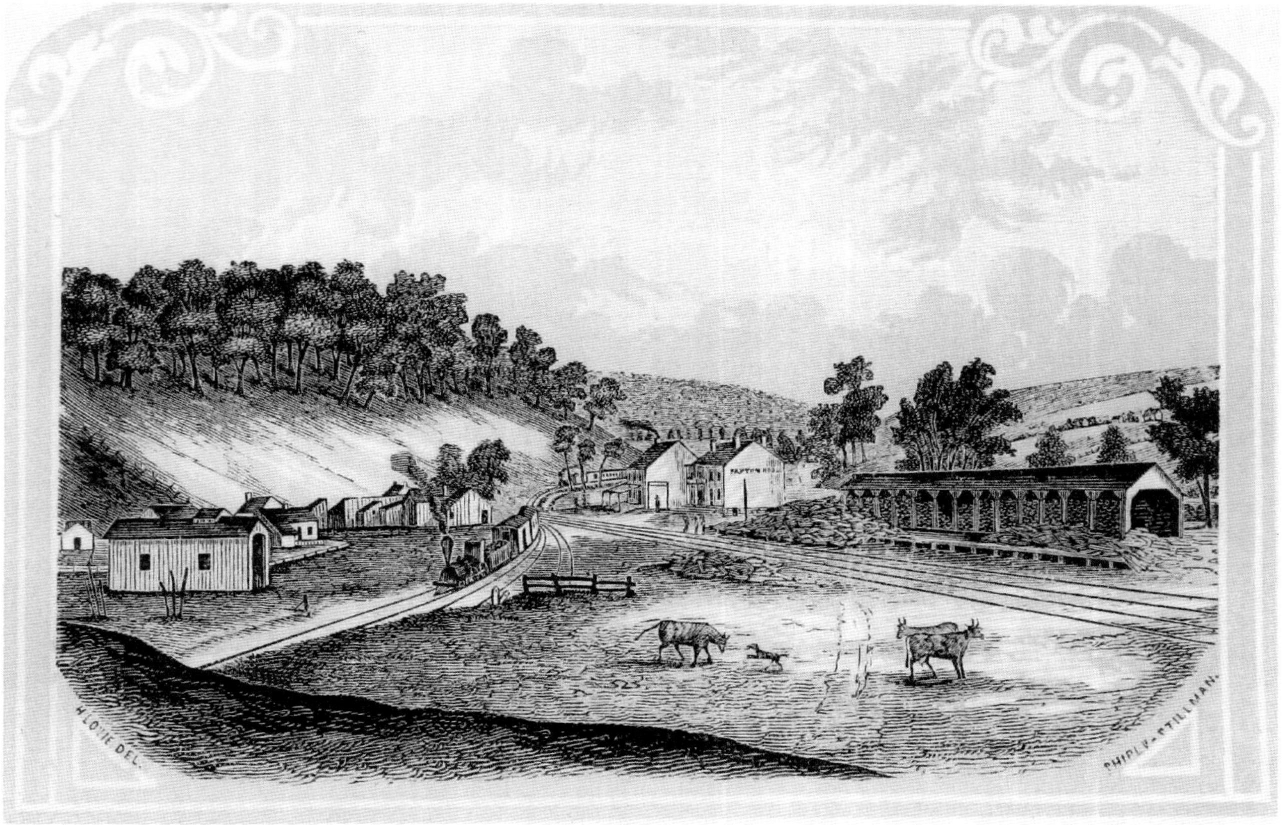

JUNCTION HILLSBOROUGH R. R. LOVELAND

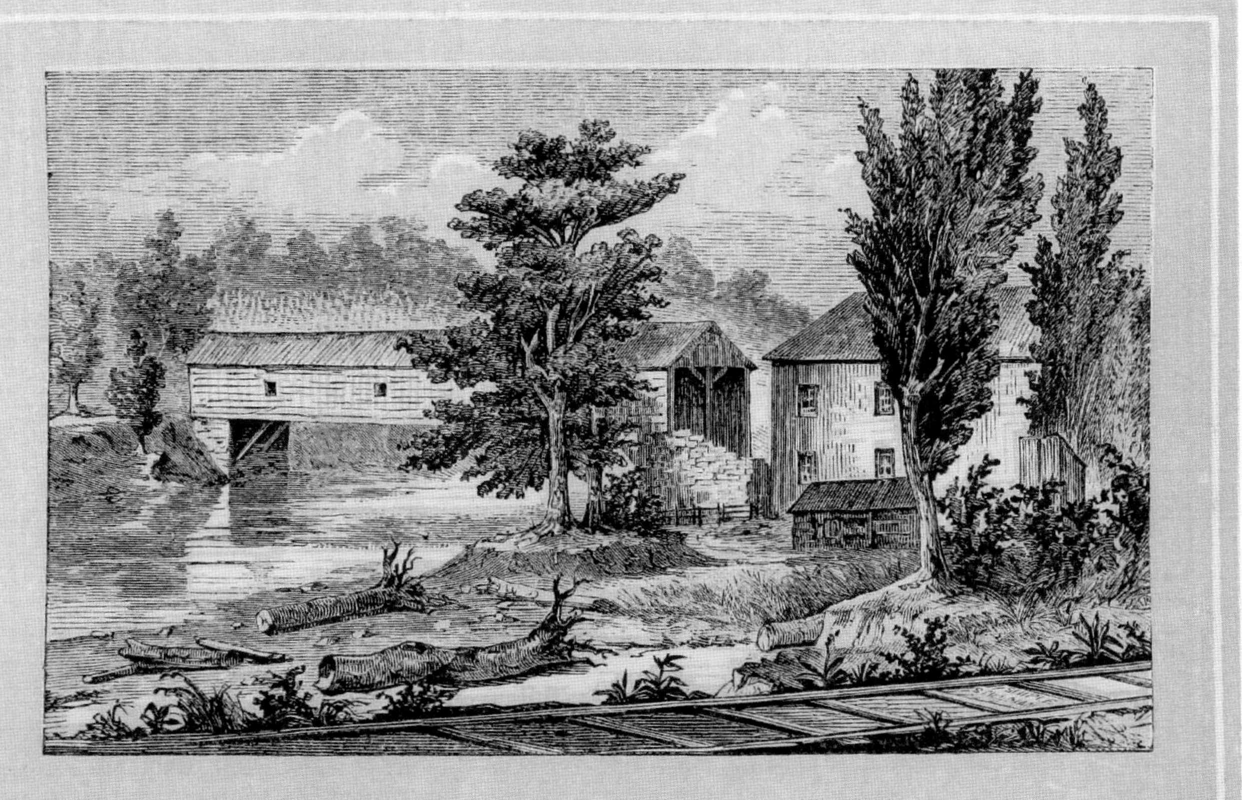

BRIDGE, MIAMI RIVER, AT FOSTER'S CROSSINGS

a house, a bridge, and a station. The Miami river is here crossed by the Montgomery turnpike, from Cincinnati to Wilmington. The situation is a very pleasant one. There are hills on both sides,—the valley being here compressed within narrow limits. The bridge, a plain simple structure, conducts to the road which you see winding up the hills on the other side. The accompanying plate represents this scene.

Just before you come to Foster's Crossings, you will notice on the left hand of the cars, as you come from Cincinnati, on the west bank of the river, a large mill and plain frame house. This was the residence of one of the real statesmen of our country—Governor MORROW. He entered public life in 1802, and remained in the public service half a century; in which time, he never once lost the public confidence, nor ever failed in any part of his duty. He was a member of the State Convention to form the first Constitution; was twelve years a member of the House of Representatives in Congress; and most of the time, the only Representative of Ohio. He was six years in the United States Senate; four years Governor; and several years, towards the close of his life, President of the Little Miami Railroad Company. He was one of the earliest friends of this enterprize, and one of the few, who *then* saw the great superiority of this mode of locomotion, and its advantages to the country. The Duke of Saxe Weimar, after visiting him in 1825, described him as a faithful copy of an ancient Cincinnatus. "He was engaged on our arrival, in cutting a wagon pole; but immediately stopped his work on our arrival, to give us a hearty welcome."

It would be well for our Republic, if the race of Morrows could be continued; if, nurtured like the mighty oaks on the soil; warmed into vigor, by the open sun; freshened by the pure air; made hardy by labor and exposure; educated to the sentiment of religion, and the love of liberty,—they could come as Morrow did—with the strength of frame; the vigor of intellect; the honest heart; and the clear eyed spirit, to the great work of Legislation. Then we should have wholesome laws, justly administered; and all selfishness and intrigue and corruption would disappear, before a fearless Patriotism. Alas! why cannot we have another era of Washingtons, and Jays, and Morrows? But, we must neither linger nor sigh, by the grave of Patriots! The cars roll on. Time flies! It is the Present only we possess.

DEERFIELD STATION.—A bridge is thrown over the river here, and the old town of Deerfield is seen on the opposite side of the river; but is now only a few scattered houses. We say *old;* for it was settled about 1797, by the Suttons, Kelly, &c. Now fifty years in Ohio, is as much as five centuries in some countries; a town which was settled fifty years ago, is looked upon as among our antiquities.

LEBANON is four miles from Deerfield, and this is the station for the Lebanon passengers to arrive at and depart from. Lebanon is the county seat of Warren county, the west side of which we are now traversing. It is noted — perhaps as much as any other county town in the United States — for its distinguished men. Among these, we may mention JOHN MCLEAN, a representative in Congress, Postmaster General, and now Judge of the Supreme Court, who commenced his career in Lebanon, as editor of the Western Star. THOMAS CORWIN, Representative in Congress, Senator, and Secretary of the Treasury, a distinguished orator, lawyer and statesman; whose father was one of the first settlers of Lebanon. THOMAS R. ROSS, representative in Congress, also an able man. JOSHUA COLLETT, the first lawyer in the county, and afterwards Judge of the Supreme Court; and Judge DUNLEVY. In fine, Lebanon and Warren county are rich in what Rome deemed her treasures — Patriots and Statesmen. Some, like MORROW, have gone to their rest; but it is hoped that the matrons of such a land, may yet be able to produce plants of so goodly a stock.

The census tells us, that Lebanon has 2,088 inhabitants. It is a pleasant retired country town.

MORROW is 36 miles from Cincinnati, and 28 from

Xenia. Morrow is one of the Railroad *creations*. It had no existence whatever, when the Railway commenced business. Now, it is a thriving and quite a well built village, with, according to the census, 458 inhabitants—but many more now; for it has much improved in the last three years. Morrow is well situated, at the mouth of Todd's Fork of the Little Miami, which, rising on the plain of Clinton county, (east) becomes here a considerable stream. You cross it near by, on a handsome wooden bridge. But Morrow will become a much larger place; for it has another advantage. It is at the intersection with the Little Miami Railroad, of the Wilmington, Circleville, and Zanesville Railroad—one of the most important lines of Railway in the country.

THE CINCINNATI, WILMINGTON AND ZANESVILLE Railroad commences at Morrow, and passing Wilmington, the county seat of Clinton County, Circleville, the county seat of Pickaway county, Washington, county seat of Fayette, and Lancaster, the county seat of Fairfield, unites with the Central Ohio Railroad at Zanesville. It thus makes a most important central line of Railway; and including 36 miles of the Little Miami Railroad, and 81 miles of the Central, will unite Wheeling and Cincinnati with a line of about 250 miles in length; the shortest route which will connect those cities. At Wheeling, oth-

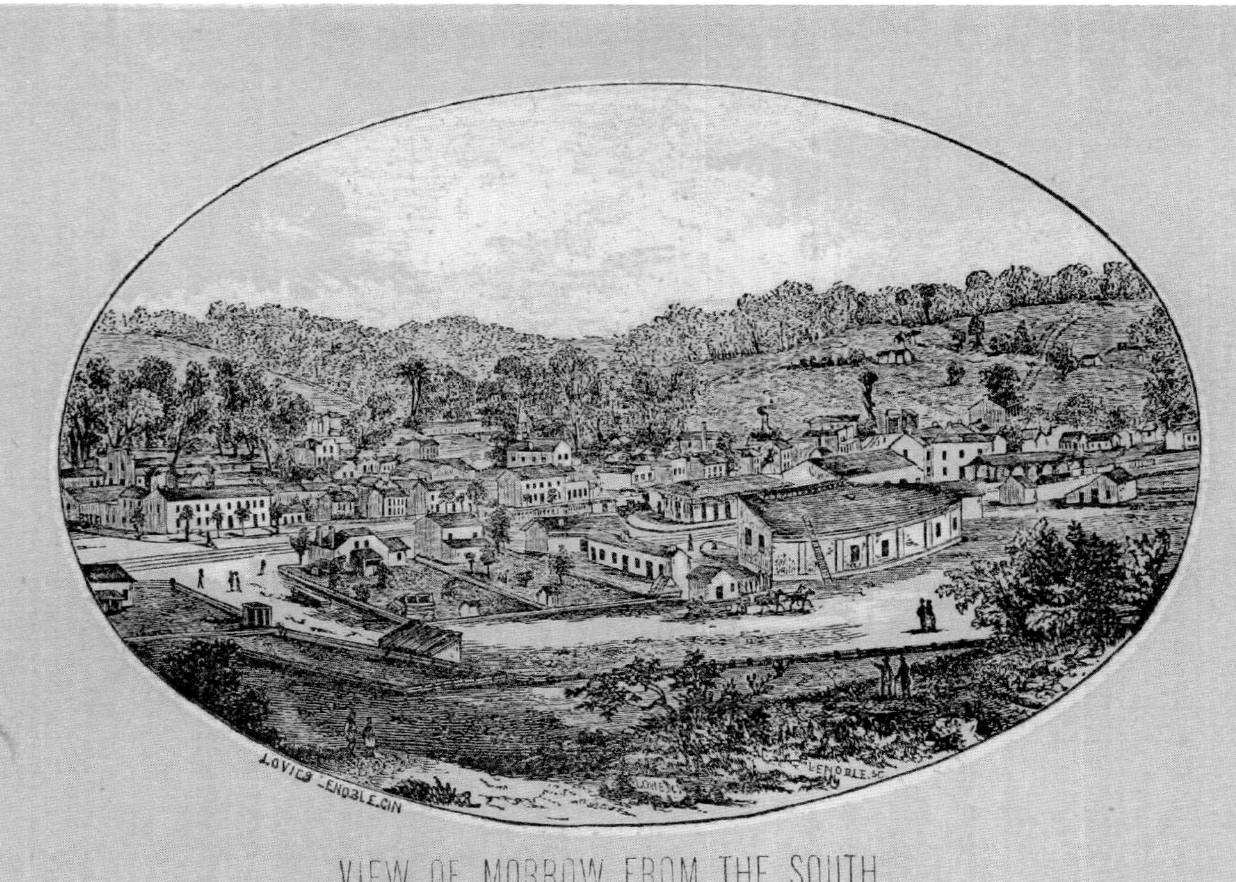

VIEW OF MORROW FROM THE SOUTH.

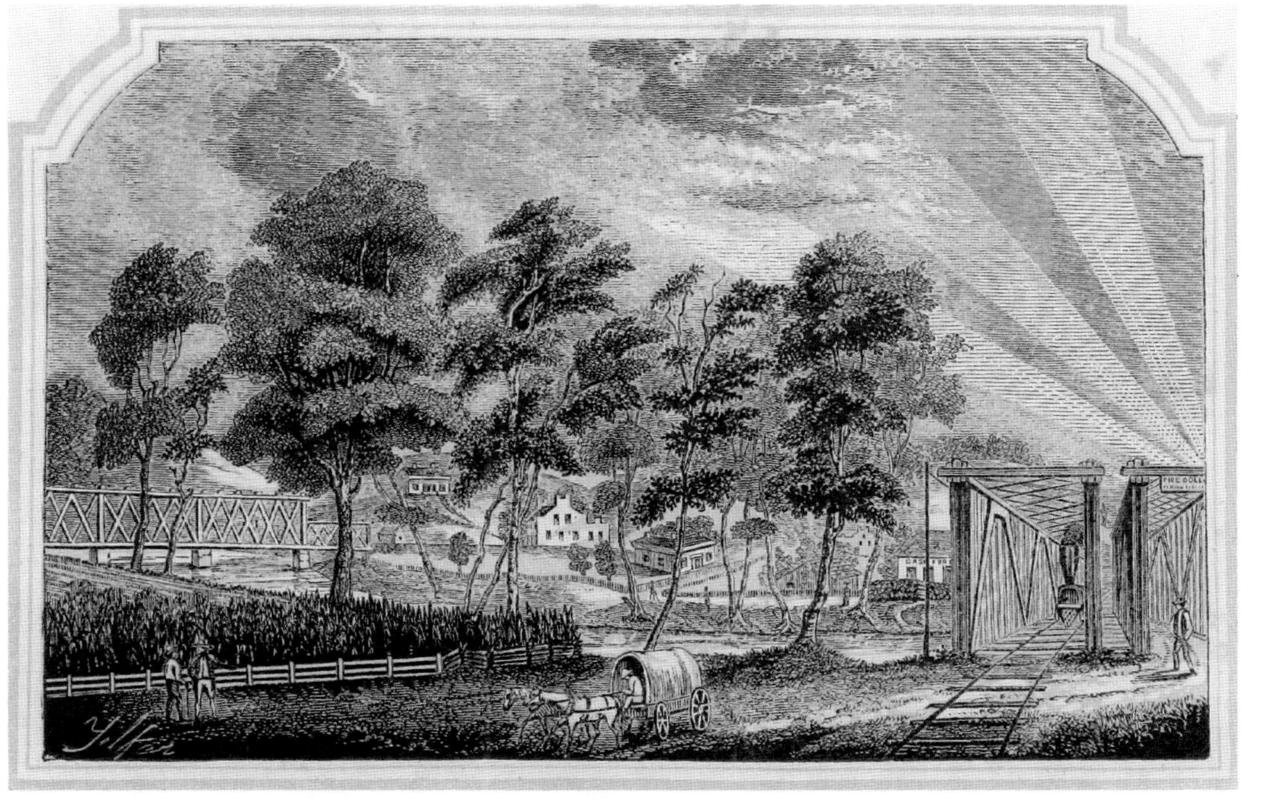

VIEW OF MORROW, FROM THE EAST.

er lines will continue the route to Baltimore and Philadelphia.

The distance from Cincinnati to the principal points on the Cincinnati, Wilmington and Zanesville line, will be nearly as follows:—

Cincinnati	to Morrow - - -	36 miles.
"	to Wilmington - -	57 "
"	to Washington - -	77 "
"	to Circleville -	105 "
"	to Lancaster - -	126 "
"	to Zanesville - -	169 "

These are all important places, in rich counties, and there is hardly a route in the Western States, which promises so much local support from the productions of the soil.

A view of Morrow, coming from the East, is on the opposite page. The bridge in front is over Todd's Fork. The Miami is on the right.

FORT ANCIENT is 41½ miles from Cincinnati, and 22½ miles from Xenia. The view is not of Fort Ancient; but of a scene on the river, a little above,—as seen from the opposite bank. Fort Ancient is on the hill above, and of course, invisible from the Railway, or the river. "And what is Fort Ancient?" says the inquisitive traveler. Ah! That is the question. It is a considerably deeper one than "Who built the Pyramid?" This Western world, especially the valley of the Mississippi, and most of all, the valley of the Ohio, contains numerous ancient monuments, some of which are unquestionably the remains of fortifications; some are evidently tombs, and others again are more doubtful; whether they were intended for military, for religious, or for monumental purposes. There are unquestionably some of each kind. Of those used for the tombs of the dead, it is questionable whether many of them were originally intended for that purpose; or, whether being found in existence, they were not used in some after generation, as ready made coffins and tombs for the dead. These tombs are called "Mounds," and are simply a raised cone of earth, with a flattened top, having the natural slope of the earth. They are of various sizes, from ten to one hundred feet in height. On some of them the largest forest trees are found; and the mounds themselves are found often in the most remote wilderness, and in the densest woods. In these mounds are almost invariably found some remains of human bones; some pottery ware; some charred ashes; and occasionally a raised altar of earth, upon which either the body was placed, or sacrifice offered. In some, as at the Grave Creek Mound, near Wheeling, there was the appearance of a regular vault, with wooden sides, prepared with something of the design and intention of the Egyptian Pyramids. Such are the "mounds" of the west. But, we come now to the important question, "were those entombed in the mounds, of the same people with those who built them? And, were those buried here, the same race with our North American Indian? And were all of them of the same race? I confess, that I incline to the last opinion. But, there is such a love of romance in the human mind, that most persons, and especially antiquarians, have loved to dwell on the idea of a mysterious people, who once inhabited this continent, and who, having built all these monuments and fortifications, were at last utterly obliterated, by a barbarous race, so that even their monuments have not preserved their name from oblivion! The strongest argument against this romantic theory is found in this last fact;—that these monuments contain nothing which furnish the slightest evidence of civilization, by which some knowledge of them might have been preserved. They were *not* a civilized people. That is certain. In fact, the builders of the mounds, and certainly those who were buried in them, were not superior at all to the better class of our North American Indians; such, for example, as the Mandans were. There is nothing in making a mound, nothing contained in them, which a tribe of Delawares or Pawnees might not have done. Where then is the mystery? As to the mounds, there is none, however much romance may make of it. By the way, here I may mention a tradition of the North Western Indians, in regard to the manner in which the mounds were formed. It may, or may not be true; but contains a very pretty idea. A chief in Wisconsin, many years since, was asked if there was no tradition of the building, or purpose of the mounds? He said that there was an old tradition, that long time ago, when a chief died, his friends and relatives laid him on a little altar, where sacrifices were made, and raised over him a hillock of earth, and that every time a friend, or a member of that tribe came by, he cast upon it a handful of earth. If he was a great chief, with a large tribe, and popular, his mound soon grew to be a large one; but if he was a small chief, his mound was small. Thus the mound marked, without an inscription, the greatness of him who lay beneath.

Now, this may have been the manner in which some mounds were formed; but they, like our own tombs, are obviously of different kinds. Some of them have been re-opened, and strangers buried in them; and others were evidently intended for religious uses; and again, others were used, as we may infer from their position, as military watch-towers.

But we must not stop you in the cars to read the history of a tomb. What, you may well ask, has this to do with Fort Ancient? Much: for there are mounds within Fort Ancient; and there are also other things, much more curious than mounds. Fort Ancient is, in fact, an old, and unknown fortification;

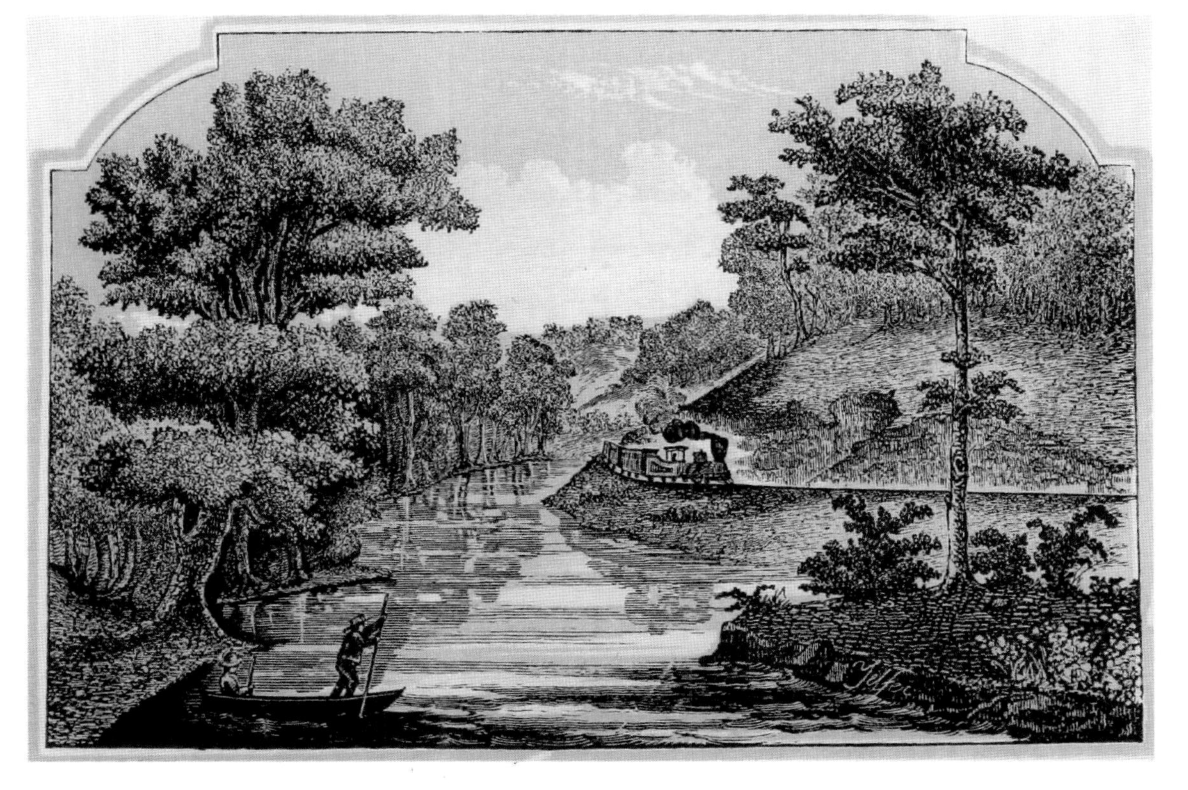

VIEW NEAR FORT ANCIENT ON THE LITTLE MIAMI RIVER.

one of the most singular of all these ancient remains which have puzzled so many. I am sorry you cannot leave the cars, and walk through it. You would see a work, most manifestly intended for defence, evidently constructed by human hands; but of whose author not the slightest trace, or memorial, or history remains, save only this solitary and deserted ruin. When you meet a ruined fortification on the Rhine, or the Danube, you know something of its authors. Its stones and walls tell you something. You can trace it very distinctly to German Barons or Roman Prætors; but here you can trace nothing. These fallen walls have no characteristics of any thing, or of any known being. They were found in a wilderness, whose wilder inhabitants knew not whence they came. There were no inscriptions. The dead had no epitaphs. The profound solitude of the woods was interrupted by no sound from its lonely tenants. There was, when first seen, around these ancient fortifications, a dreary and painful solitude; a sense of presence, and yet a death-like repose. I recollect well a feeling of awe, when I first passed through Fort Ancient. The mounds seemed as if they would speak, and just then a huge black snake drew himself across the road, as if he were the genius of the place. I dare say no such impression is produced now; for all around is cultivation, and the air of life and activity pervades the neighborhood.

Of Fort Ancient, the description in brief is this: It stands on a plain, about 230 feet above the river, and between two rivulets running into the Miami. Each of these streams has high and steep banks; so that, in fact, this position is defended naturally, on three sides. It is only open on the fourth, or east side. The plain is nearly level, and on it is erected an irregular fortification, generally following the bank of the river and the creeks, in the shape of a high parapet, on the water side about eight or ten feet high, but on the plain nearly double that. To this parapet there are gateways, mounds, and some exterior defences. Nothing is more obvious, than that the work was intended for defence; and it is equally certain, that the position was selected with skill and sagacity. If a modern general was to select some spot on the Miami river to defend, he could not have chosen a better one.

But I have detained you here long enough. We must hasten on. The railway runs at the base of the hills, and therefore shuts from sight all these ancient memorials. To a curious and contemplative mind, these remains are very interesting, and weeks might be occupied in examining these and similar monuments on the Miami, and Scioto. The view accompanying this is not of Fort Ancient, but of a scene on the Little Miami river, above the fort; in my opinion quite beautiful.

CORWIN, 50 miles from Cincinnati, and 14 from Xenia, is a station opposite the pretty town of Waynesville, Warren county, Ohio. On a clear day you will see across the Miami, (over which a bridge is thrown,) a village of white houses, lying amidst the foliage of a green slope. It is to my eye one of the most rural and beautiful towns, as seen from the station, any where to be found. It has no ambition to be a busy manufacturing or mercantile place; and therefore you see no dark columns of smoke, no tall chimneys, no din of noise. All is quiet, serene, rural and retired. By the way, there is one branch of business carried on here, the traveler may as well know. There is here a maker of Maple-sugar Candy, who unquestionably makes the best in the nation. If you see him in the cars, with his little boxes, five chances to one you will say "no." For you will think of the half-flour, musty stuff, you generally find under the name of candy. All I have to say, is, that this is real maple candy, the best in the country.

Waynesville is not *pretentious*. It is simply a rural village, originally settled by Quakers, and like them quiet, and unobtrusive. By the census, it has 744 inhabitants. There are two Friends' Meeting houses, and a Methodist Church.

SPRING VALLEY, 57 miles from Cincinnati, and 7 miles from Xenia, is a pleasant village; small, but neat. There is a woolen factory, a tavern, several shops, and in the neighborhood, a good many mills, and factories. The turnpike from Cincinnati to Xenia also passes here. The land is rich, the Miami river near by; so that on the whole, this position is a very good one, for those who wish to live in the country, and yet be in a village. It is called Spring Valley, from the very peculiar nature of the hills, and soil around. The hills which surround the place are full of springs, which gush out, almost as large as rivulets. For two or three miles, they are almost innumerable. You will see them on the slopes, as we pass up the little valley of Glady. This is the name of the little stream, we now follow to Xenia. Glady is only seven miles in length, rising in some large springs, near Xenia. In that seven miles, however, it turns the wheels of some seven or eight mills and factories. It is the busiest little water course you ever saw.

When you get half way through this valley, about three miles from Xenia, in the woods on the left, is the spot where Daniel Boone made his escape from the Indians. He had been taken prisoner by the Indians, and carried to Old Chillicothe, now called "Old Town," which is about six miles beyond this place, on the Miami. At Old Town he found a large body of Indians, painted and armed, ready for an attack on Booneborough, his own place. There he determined to fly, and on the morning of the 18th of

June, 1778, being left on Glady, near this spot, with only an old Indian and two women, he took himself off, and made a straight line for Booneborough. It was well he did; for he found the fort in bad repair, and went to work at once, to put it in order.

This region around "Old Chillicothe," and from thence on, and to the Scioto, was the residence of the Shawnese, once one of the greatest and best of the Indian tribes. The Shawnees were originally residents of the South; but, (says Col. John Johnston,) came to Ohio long anterior to Braddock's campaign in 1754. They occupied the country contiguous to the Wyandots, on the Scioto, Mad River, and Great Miami, and the upper waters of the Maumee. They were devoted friends and allies of the Wyandots, in all their wars with the whites. These two tribes were the last to leave Ohio, and there is not now an Indian, who owns an acre of land within the State. "Alas! the poor Indian!" says some one. Yes, my friend, and alas! the poor white! For, the Indian was only a savage, and he made war upon the whites, as the whites did upon wolves and bears; and many were the poor women and children who were tomahawked and scalped, in their ferocious rage. You will say, perhaps, the Indians *owned* the land; are you quite sure of that? Investigate. These Shawnees were only wanderers. They came on to the land once occupied by the Wyandots. Did the

Wyandots own it? No. They came where the Delawares and Iroquois once owned. In fine, can any wandering, savage tribe *own* a country, which they do not even occupy? but in which they are vagabonds and wanderers? They are unquestionably entitled to the rights of life, liberty and labor; but, *ownership*, according to the civilized idea of property, they had none.

XENIA is 64 miles from Cincinnati, and 54 miles from Columbus. It is the county seat of Greene county, and one of the best inland towns of the west. But before we discuss the town, let us discuss another, and quite a practical question. At least *you* will think it so. Are you hungry? Is this supper time? If so, let me tell you, of all the railway depots in the United States, this is one of the best for a meal. It is clean, roomy, and the meals are well got by friend Stark, and charged for no more, than they ought to be. In all the New York and Pennsylvania railways, there is not a place better than this to get a nice supper. So if you are hungry and will be satisfied with good things, and don't demand ortolans and turbot out of season, now is your chance. Sit down and be comforted.

Now, if you have done supper, we will take a look at Xenia. *Xenia*, where did they get that name? I cannot tell. I have heard something of its origin, but really cannot trace it to any known thing. Well,

Xenia contains 4,248 inhabitants, just treble what it did in 1840, and twelve hundred more than it did in 1850. This shows a rapid growth, and it is due almost entirely to the railways which here intersect. The Little Miami, on which we now are, passes on north to join the Mad River road, at Springfield; while on the east it is connected with Columbus, by the Xenia and Columbus, on which we shall now proceed. Xenia township is the largest township in Ohio, and contains about 8,500 inhabitants. It was settled chiefly by the Seceders, as they were called, the Covenanters of the Associate Reformed Church, all of whom are branches of the same sect, the old Scotch Covenanters. In the town of Xenia, there are now twelve churches, of which *one* is Seceder, *one* Covenanter, *two* Associate Reformed, *two* Methodist, *one* Presbyterian, *one* Baptist, *one* German Lutheran, *one* Roman Catholic, and *two* African. This is more than a church to each 400 people. So you see this is a church going people. In the county there are 65 churches, or one to each 300 persons, a very large proportion. In general, Greene county is settled by a sober, industrious, orderly, and intelligent people. You would readily see this from the very look of the farms, if you could see them. Generally, however, our railways do not pass through the most cultivated sections.

But, to return to Xenia: we shall not see it nearer

than at the depot. But, even here, the town bears a pleasant aspect, bright and thriving. The little stream that separates us from town is SHAWNEE, which runs as clear and bright, as if it were leaping over the rocks and sands of New England. Its name is the only thing in this broad land, except those strange old mounds, which reminds us of the ancient inhabitants. Shawnee! Dost thou still remember the Shawnee, the wild warrior of the forest, who once roamed upon thy banks, and hunted in thy woods,—and frolicked in the loud joy of a freeman?

Again we start, and soon we shall leave thee, fair Xenia, behind, and bid farewell to all thy charms, thy spires, thy woods and waters! Of none can it be more truly said, than of thee,—

"————Loveliest village of the plain,
Where health and plenty cheer the lab'ring swain,
Where smiling Spring its earliest visit pays,
And parting Summer's ling'ring bloom delays.

How often have I paused on every charm,
The shelter'd cot, the cultivated farm,
The never failing brook, the busy mill,
The decent church that tops the neighb'ring hill."

We pass near,—but shall not see,—TAWAWA SPRINGS, a fashionable summer resort for the citizens of Cincinnati. This is a new place, being established only within four or five years. Originally, it was a beautiful piece of wood, or rolling land, in the midst of which was a deep ravine. In that ravine arose

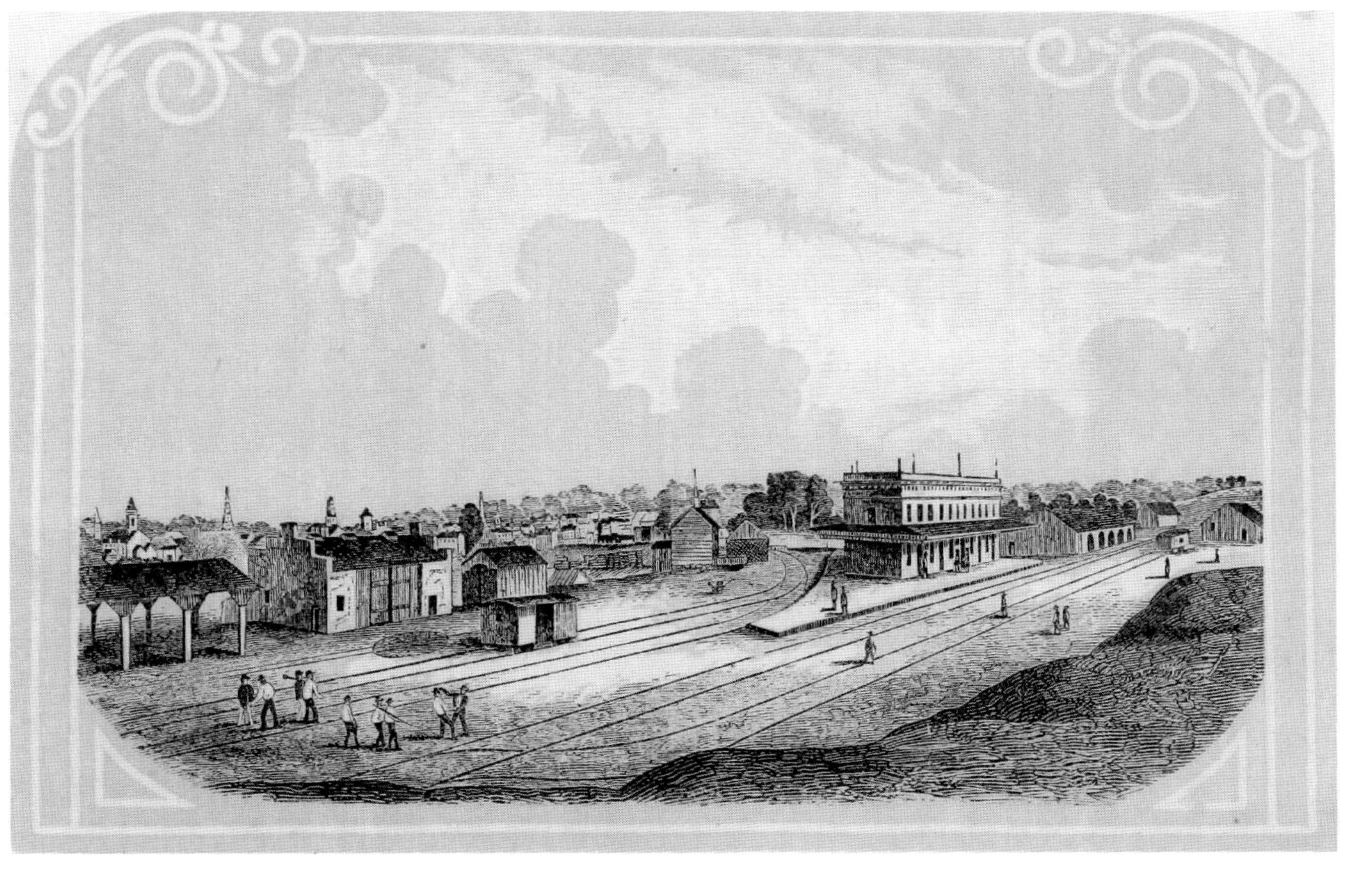

VIEW OF STATION HOUSE AT XENIA.

three springs; one was pure natural water; one was lime-water, and one was iron and sulphur. The beauty of the situation, with the presence of the springs, gave to Mr. E. F. Drake, who first started the enterprize, the idea of making it a watering place. This has been accomplished, and TAWAWA is now both a beautiful, and a fashionable place. A large, elegant, and most comfortable hotel has been erected; in front of which is a lawn, shaded by forest trees. On each side are rows of cottages, most of them erected by gentlemen for their own families. The roads around Xenia are very good and pleasant for riding; the country remarkably healthy; the place accessible, at the Xenia Railway station, from every part of the United States. In thirty hours you can be in New York, or Philadelphia, from Tawawa Springs! In two hours you can be in Cincinnati. I have been at most of the watering places in this country, and I assure you, that for comfort with seclusion, and convenience with pleasure, there is not another place in the United States, more comfortable, convenient and pleasant than this. A fine view of Xenia, and the depot accompanies this.

CEDARVILLE Station, 72 miles from Cincinnati, and 46 from Columbus. There occurs here rather a remarkable natural phenomenon for this country,—the presence of Cedar trees,—and hence the name of the village,—Cedarville. The village is seen from the left, through a clump of trees. It is situated at the Falls of Massie's Creek, a stream quite celebrated in Indian wars, and Indian adventures. The Falls of Massie's Creek was quite a romantic spot, the waters plunging over rock precipices, and overhung by darkly green cedars. But, alas! the cedars are cut away; the red Indian has disappeared; there is no more danger; and quiet people plant corn and tend sheep! Wild wars and fearful romance have disappeared forever! Not even the spirit-rappers can recall them.

SELMA Station, 6 miles further, is a new place, created by the Railroad.

SOUTH CHARLESTON Station, 83 miles from Cincinnati and 35 miles from Columbus, is another small country village, in a very pleasant country. After passing Cedarville, we enter upon a country which in its scenery, soil, and qualities, is quite peculiar. It comprehends about one fourth of Ohio. Commencing in the upper part of Highland county, including a small part of Clark, (where we are now,) and all of Fayette, Madison, Union, Hardin, Wyandot, Crawford, and parts of Marion, Huron, Logan, Champaign and several other counties; it extends from the hills of the Ohio, to near the shores of the lake. It may be called, generally, a *champaign* country, nearly level, but with gentle swells like the waves of the sea, interspersed with natural prairies, and clumps of wood. The small quantity of timber, and the apparent absence of fertile "bottoms," (the favorites of all good farmers,) induced the pioneers to give these lands the name "barrens;" but, nothing was more mistaken than to attach to them the word *barren*. They are among the most fertile, as well as the most beautiful lands in America. Being peculiarly adapted to grass, they have heretofore been chiefly employed in grazing sheep and cattle. In the township where we now are, great numbers of sheep are raised. The county of Clark, in which we are, has 50,000 sheep and 12,000 cattle, most of which are pastured at this end of the county.

Charleston is a small, but pleasant village; one of those country settlements of which there are numbers in every section.

The Railway from Xenia to Columbus, we should have said, is almost entirely straight, making but three curves, we believe, in the whole distance: one on leaving Xenia, one at London, where the general direction of the road is changed, and one between there and Columbus. From Xenia to Columbus bridge, an *air line* is 52 miles; while the railway is only 54 miles, showing how near an air line this road is.

LONDON, 94 miles from Cincinnati, and 24 miles from Columbus, is the county seat of Madison county. On the next page is a view of the depot, and station house. Before we reach here, we cross a little stream, which deserves to be mentioned, because it is one of the sources of Deer Creek, a tributary of the Scioto, which it joins about seven miles above Chillicothe. The valley of Deer Creek is very fertile, and its bottoms produce an immense quantity of corn.

London is a small town of, perhaps, 500 inhabitants. The country here has the same general charteristics we have described. Madison county, of which it is the seat of justice, is not very populous; nor can it be, till the lands are subdivided. Being a grazing country, the farms are of great size; many of them being a thousand acres, and upwards. Cattle are here the leading product. Of these upwards of 20,000 are owned in the county; and in the grazing season, many more are pastured. The young cattle are bought by the graziers in Illinois, Missouri, and the far west; and they are pastured and fed on the stock farms of the Scioto, and its tributaries. These broad champaign lands afford the pasture, and the corn crops of the Scioto, Paint, Darby and Deer Creek, the corn for fattening. Feeding cattle in Ohio is a lucrative branch of farming.

SPRINGFIELD AND LONDON RAILROAD, 19 miles to Springfield. At this point, the Springfield Railroad intersects the Xenia and Columbus R. R. This link unites several important lines. It makes a connec-

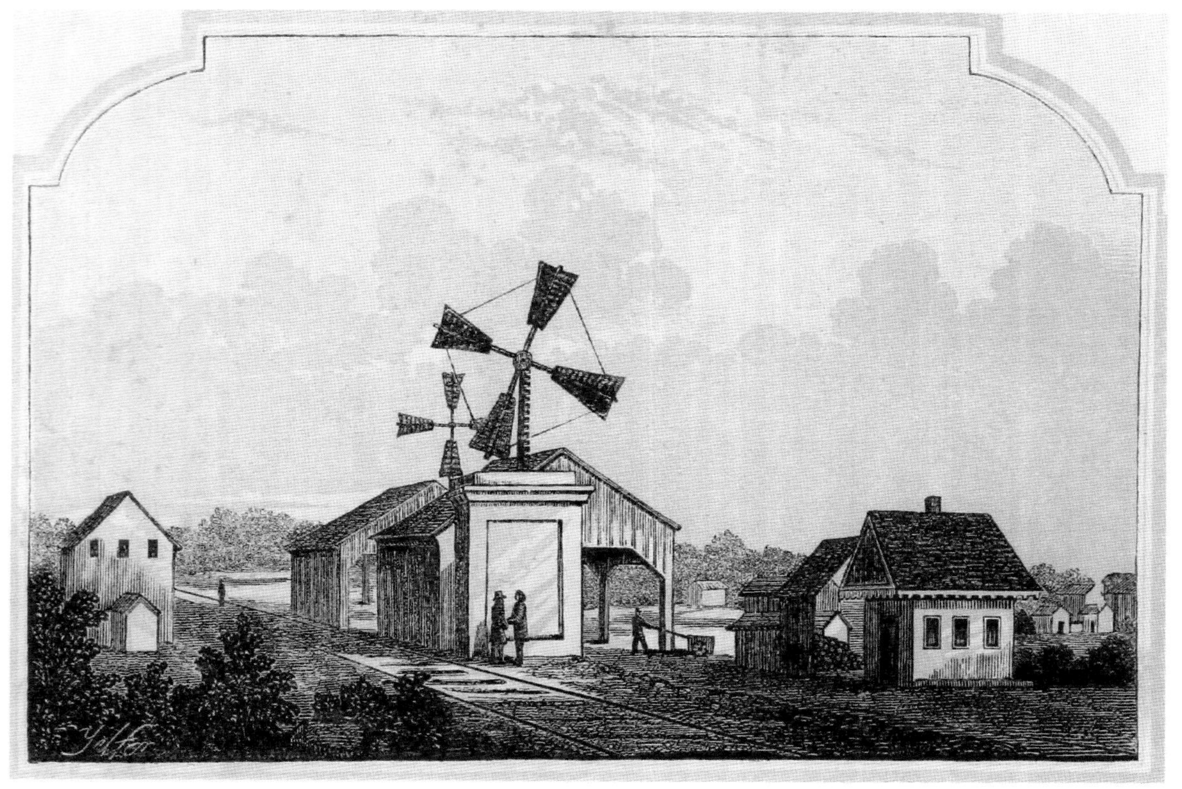

LONDON, MADISON CO

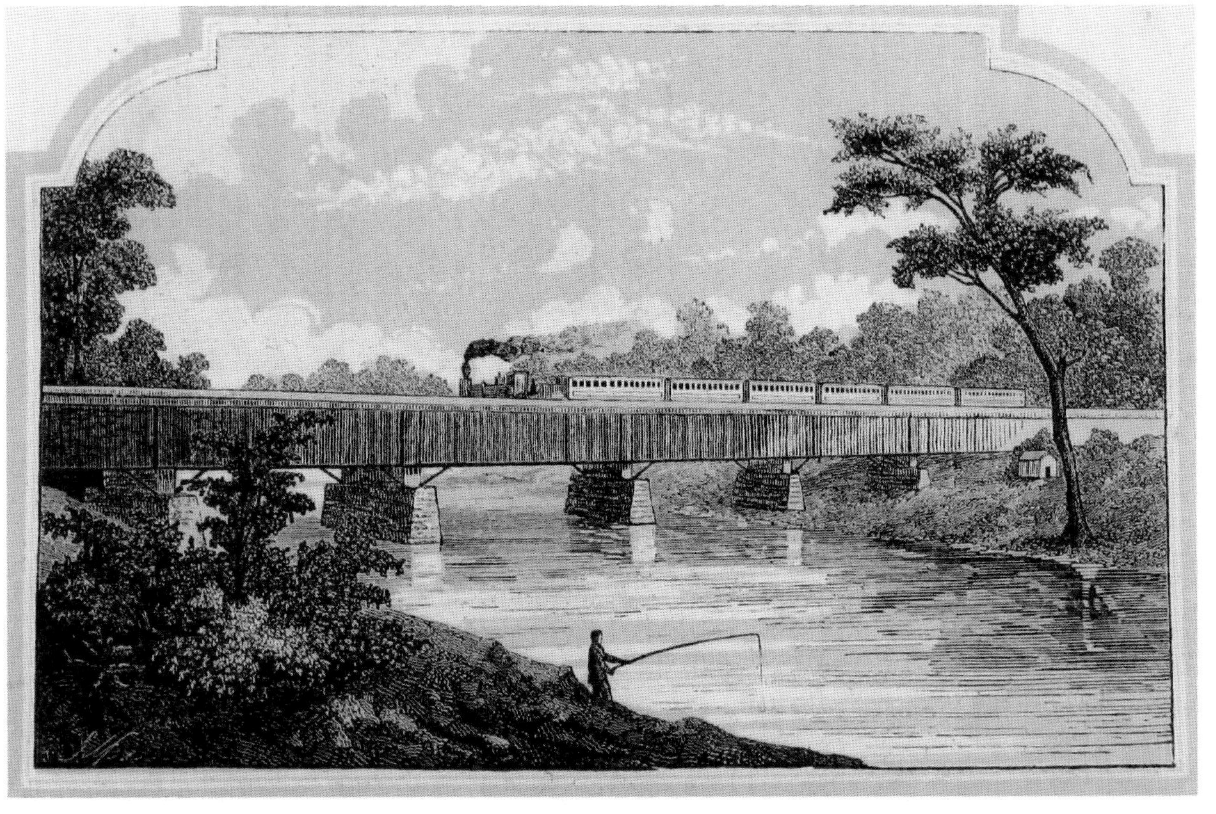

BRIDGE OVER BIG DARBY ON C. AND X. R. R.

tion between Springfield and Columbus 43 miles, and at Springfield it connects with the Mad River and Lake Erie R. R., which northwardly proceeds to Sandusky, and southwardly to Dayton. At Dayton the connection is made *via* the Greenville and Indianapolis line, with Central Indiana, *via* the Western R. R., and the Central Indiana R. R., with Richmond and Indianapolis; and *via* the Cincinnati, Hamilton, and Dayton, with Cincinnati. This short link is, therefore, both convenient and important.

BRIDGE OVER BIG DARBY CREEK, near West Jefferson. A plate of the Bridge and Creek may be seen on the opposite page. It is unfortunate for travelers that they see very little of the scenery represented in the plates, while they are in the cars. One must be below, in the valleys of streams, on the sides of hills, and under the bridges, to see the real scenery of the country, and enjoy it. The general aspect of the country, however green and rich, at certain seasons, is tame and monotonous; yet along the bank of Darby may be found some beautiful scenery.

DARBY CREEK, we must beg leave to bring more distinctly to your notice, and revive, O! Traveler, some of your historical recollections. Historical recollections, in this new country? you will say. Yes! and old recollections too of by gone times, and memorable men. Let us walk a little together, by the bank of Darby. About thirty miles below this,

Darby creek flows into the Scioto, nearly opposite the town of Circleville. Below the mouth of Darby, on the Scioto, the country is called the Darby Plains, broad, fertile, beautiful lands. On the Darby plains, four miles below Darby, where now is the village of West Fall, stood one of the Shawnee towns called "Old Chillicothe." And there stood the cabin of LOGAN. Have I not awakened your curiosity? In America, who has not heard of Logan? With nothing but his character to sustain him, he has made an immortal name, amidst the renowned of the earth. He was one of nature's noblemen, and has taken a place, which no factitious rank could have conferred. "But *who*," some stranger may say, "was Logan?" Let us pause awhile to hear the story of Logan. He was a Mingo Chief, and is thus described by John Heckewelder, the Moravian Missionary.

"LOGAN was the second son of SHIKELLAMUS, a celebrated chief of the Cayuga nation. This chief had a strong attachment to the English Government, and having the confidence of the Six Nations, was very useful in settling disputes, &c. His residence was at Shamokin, where he took great delight in acts of hospitality towards the whites. He was visited in 1742, at his residence, by Count Zinzendorf, to whom his name and fame were made known.

In 1772, says Heckewelder, "Logan was introduced to me by an Indian friend, as a son of the late chief

Shikellamus. In the course of conversation, I thought him a man of superior talents to the Indians generally. The subject turning on vice and immorality, he confessed his too great share of it, especially a fondness for liquor. He censured the whites for imposing liquor on the Indians, but admired their ingenuity; spoke of gentlemen, but observed, the Indians unfortunately had too few of them for neighbors; spoke of his friendship for the whites, and intention to settle on the Ohio, below Big Beaver; and invited me to visit him. I was then living at the Moravian Towns. In April, 1773, while on my passage down the Ohio, from the Muskingum, I called at Logan's settlement, where I received every civility I could expect from such of the family as were at home."

At this time, Logan was living at or near Yellow Creek, Ohio. In the following year, (spring of 1774) according to the testimony of Ebenezer Zane, a Captain Michael Cresap attacked and killed two Indians. The next day, Cresap and Greathouse, with a party of men, fell upon and killed another party of Indians, at Grave Creek, below Wheeling. Within a few days after, Greathouse's party killed other Indians at Yellow Creek. In these several unprovoked murders, the brother, sister, and all the family of Logan were killed; so that this friend of the whites was left alone in the world, with all kindred cut off, by those who should have been his protectors.

With such provocations and such barbarous cruelty on the part of his dearest friends, was it strange the red warrior felt the spirit of vengeance? The last affair had taken place on the 24th of May, 1774; and on the 12th of July, Logan, with a few warriors, had reached the settlement of the Monongahela; where his first attack was on three men pulling flax in a field. One was shot, and the two others taken. These two—one of whom was a Mr. Robinson—were taken to the Indian Town, where, according to the usages of the Indians, they would have to run the gauntlet, and then be burned, if not adopted into some Indian family. But Logan delighted not in torture. In the most friendly spirit he told Robinson how to escape the severities of the gauntlet. At last, however, he was tied to a stake, and would have been burned; but Logan insisted on his being adopted, cut the cords with his own hands, put a belt of wampum upon him, and pointed out an old woman, who was henceforth to be his aunt. He was adopted instead of a warrior, killed at Yellow Creek.

These events gave rise to a most terrible Indian war, which was finally terminated, by a decisive battle at Point Pleasant, mouth of the Kenhawa. There, the Shawanese, Mingoes and Delawares, were defeated by the Virginia militia. The Indians sued for peace. But LOGAN disdained to be among the suppliants. But—lest the sincerity of the treaty should be doubted—when so distinguished a chief was absent, he sent to Lord Dunmore his celebrated speech. The genuineness of this speech has been fully established by the most abundant testimony. It was delivered (according to Judge Gibson of Pittsburgh), in the fall of 1774, when Dunmore's army had reached within fifteen miles of "Old Chillicothe," (now Westfall) where Logan then lived. A flag came out to request an interview with some one, sent in by Dunmore. Gibson, who could speak three languages, went in, and to him Logan delivered his speech for Lord Dunmore. It was delivered, after shedding many tears—a proof of the depth of feeling with which it was attended. It was so remarkable, as to strike everybody; and was immediately published in the American Colonies, and throughout Europe. It became the theme of wonder, and the exercise of schools in eloquence; and has ever since been perpetuated as an example of oratory for youth. The correct edition of his speech is the following:

"I appeal to any white man to say, if ever he entered Logan's cabin hungry, and he gave him not meat; if ever he came cold and naked, and he clothed him not. During the course of the last long and bloody war, Logan remained idle in his cabin, an advocate for peace. Such was my love for the whites, that my countrymen pointed, as they passed, and said, 'Logan is the friend of white men.' I had even thought to have lived with you, but for the injuries of one man. Colonel Cresap, the last spring, in cold blood, and unprovoked, murdered all the relations of Logan, not even sparing my women and children. There runs not a drop of my blood in the veins of any living creature. This called on me for revenge. I have sought it. I have killed many. I have glutted my vengeance. For my country, I rejoice in the beams of peace. But do not harbor a thought that mine is the joy of fear. Logan never felt fear. He will not turn on his heel to save his life. Who is there to mourn for Logan? Not one."

The authenticity of this speech is proved, as I have said, by the testimony of Gibson to the delivery of it, and by abundance of other testimony to all the material facts.

The close of Logan's life does not seem to be known with certainty The Indians reported, says Heckewelder, that after the peace, he fell into a deep melancholy. "Life," he said, "had become a torment to him, and he knew no more what pleasure was; and he thought he had better never have existed." The single expression, "Who is there to mourn for Logan?" carries with it the very depth of melancholy. Nor is it strange. The heart of the poor Indian was as tender as other hearts — and by fell murder, wife, children, and friends were taken from him forever. Who was there to mourn for Logan?

The Indians said he became delirious, and went to Detroit, drank freely, and was murdered between that place and Miami. This story, however, is doubtful. In the "American Pioneer," it is said that he died of disease, in "Old Chillicothe,"—on the very spot where he delivered his renowned speech.

And now we must return up the Darby. The cars are flying fast. These broad plains will soon be gone, and Logan and his memory be effaced from our minds. Very near where we are now, lived JONATHAN ALDER, who was brought up entirely among the Indians. He was captured in 1782, near Greenbriar, Va., and was saved only by the circumstance of his having black hair, which induced his Indian captor to think he would make a very good Indian. He was adopted into the family of an Indian chief of the Mingo tribe, who had lost a son in battle.

Jonathan lived with Mary—a daughter of the chief—who had become the wife of Col. Lewis, another chief. He says they treated him with the utmost kindness, and exclaims, "Oh! never have I, nor can I express the affection I had for these two persons." Of their mode of living, he says, "I would have lived very happy, if I could have had my health; but for three or four years, I was subject to very severe attacks of fever and ague. Their diet went very hard with me for a long time. Their chief living was meat and hominy; but we rarely had bread, and very little salt, which was extremely scarce and dear, as well as milk and butter. Honey and sugar were plenty, and used a great deal in their cooking, as well as on their food.

Alder was with the Indians at the time of Crawford's defeat, and at the Mackachack towns, when destroyed by Logan; and remained with the Indians till after Wayne's victory in 1795. When he grew up, he took a squaw for wife, and lived on Darby creek. When the settlers began to come there, he learned to speak English, and soon began to farm like the whites. He kept hogs, cows, and horses, sold milk and butter to the Indians, and accumulated property. Finally, Alder found, from some of the settlers, where his mother and brothers lived; returned to them, and like Joseph, made himself known. At last, he separated from his Indian wife, and henceforth lived like the whites.

In Alder, we see a strong illustration of the differences in races, as to habits and modes of life. The moment Alder—who was nothing but an Indian in his education—saw the white settlers farming and cultivating the soil, he did the same, and accumulated property by industry. The Indians might have done the same. Why did they not? This is the precise difference. If the Indians had even been

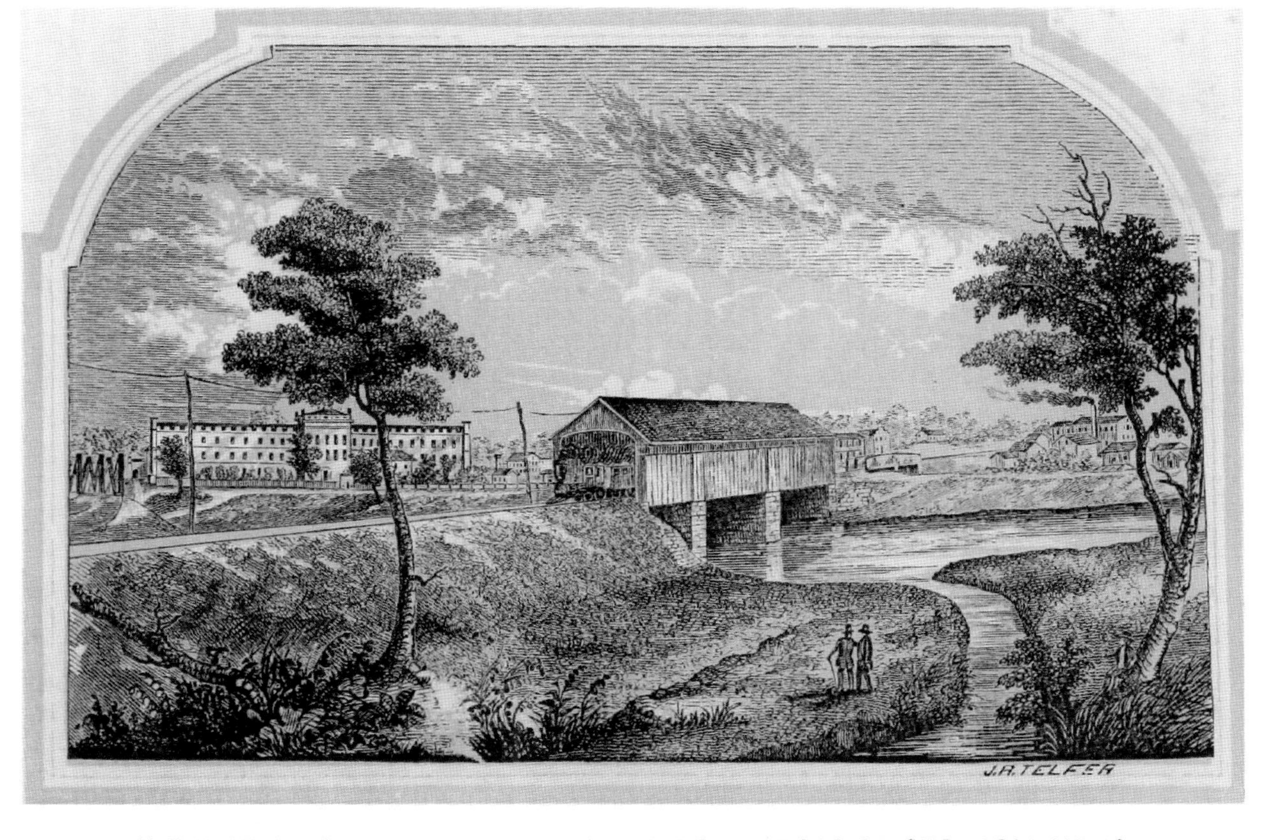

VIEW OF OHIO PENITENTIARY AND BRIDGE ACROSS SCIOTO, COLUMBUS.

able or willing to cultivate the soil, they would have been civilized. But they did not. We cannot account for these things, unless there is some secret instinct, which, by impelling them to different families and tribes, impels them also to different destinies.

FRANKLINTON, 118 miles from Cincinnati, and opposite Columbus. This now old village, was laid out many years before Columbus; but, as you see, is on low ground, and by no means so well adapted for a town. It was laid out in August, 1797, by Lucas Sullivant, and was the first settlement in the county. For several years, there was no mill or post office nearer than Chillicothe, about 45 miles. In the first years of its settlement, it was like all other new places—especially on very rich soil—extremely sickly, with the fever and ague. But with the cultivation of the land, and the better mode of living, the disease gradually disappeared; and the site of Columbus and the adjacent country is now quite healthy.

COLUMBUS, the seat of Government for the State of Ohio, is 118 miles from Cincinnati, and 135 miles from Cleveland. We approach it by a bridge over the Scioto, with the Penitentiary in view, on the left.

THE SCIOTO RIVER is one of the principal streams in the State, and interlocks near the borders of Logan county, with the head waters of the Little Miami, up which we ascended by the Little Miami Railroad 60 miles. Since then, we have passed over the elevated plain, which divides the valleys of these streams. We came on to the waters of the Scioto 40 miles west of Columbus, and have since been in what geologists call the valley of the Scioto. The district of land between the Scioto and Little Miami, is called the "Virginia Military District." This was a body of land granted by Congress to the officers and soldiers of the Virginia line, in the revolutionary war. These lands were "located," as it is called, under warrants issued by the State of Virginia. As each man employed his own surveyor, and selected his own land, the result was a great deal of confusion; but fortunately for the State of Ohio, much less than in the State of Kentucky. The lands of the Military District are probably among the best in the United States. As the warrants were bought by "locators," surveyors, etc., from the original owners, this section of country became the scene of great speculation.

The Scioto valley, so called, comprehends in all, 7,000 square miles, about the size of the State of Massachusetts, and 350,000 inhabitants. The majority of the settlers were from Virginia and Kentucky, and have given to this region many of their peculiar characteristics.

Columbus is on the east bank of the Scioto, in the midst of the broad and beautiful plain, which constitutes the central and western portion of Ohio. The land in Franklin county was once the property of the Wyandot Indians. They had a large town here, and cultivated extensive fields of corn, where Franklinton now is. It is a curious fact, that all the considerable towns, which have grown up in the valley of the Ohio, are on the site of old Indian towns. It proves the sagacity of the Indians to be quite equal to that of the whites in this particular. It shows, also, that there are natural advantages in some places, for towns and cities, which cannot be overlooked. Just before Columbus was settled by the whites, it was the scene of a singular Indian tragedy, whose cause was not unfamiliar to the history of the whites, and shows that frail human nature is everywhere the same, however the habits and aptitudes of races may differ. The *cause* of the tragedy was a charge of witchcraft!

The unfortunate subject of this charge was a Wyandot chief, called Leatherlips; and he was executed for the supposed crime of witchcraft, which seems to be outlawed in all countries. In June, 1810, Leatherlips was encamped on the Scioto, twelve miles above the present Columbus, where he was visited by six Wyandots, who, General Harrison said, were direct from Tippecanoe, by the orders of Tecumthe, and his brother, the Prophet. Sentence of death had been pronounced upon Leatherlips, when some whites, who were present, made an effort to save his life; but in vain. A council was held. The warriors spoke with warmth and bitterness; and he replied calmly and dispassionately. He was a second time condemned and soon executed. When sentence was again pronounced, the prisoner walked slowly to his camp; ate his dinner of jerked venison; arrayed himself in his best apparel, and painted his face. His dress was very rich, his hair gray, and his whole appearance graceful and commanding. When the hour of execution arrived, he shook hands in silence with the spectators. Then turning from his wigwam, with a voice of surpassing strength and melody, he commenced the chant of the death song. He was followed close by the Wyandot warriors, all timing with their slow and measured march, the music of his wild and melancholy dirge. The white men, too, joined, as silent followers, in that strange procession. At the distance of eighty yards from the camp, they came to a shallow grave, which had already been prepared. Here the old man knelt down, and in a solemn and elevated voice, addressed his prayer to the Great Spirit! Then the captain of the Indians knelt down, and prayed in a similar manner,—the prayers of both being in the Wyandot tongue.

There was not a weapon of any kind to be seen in

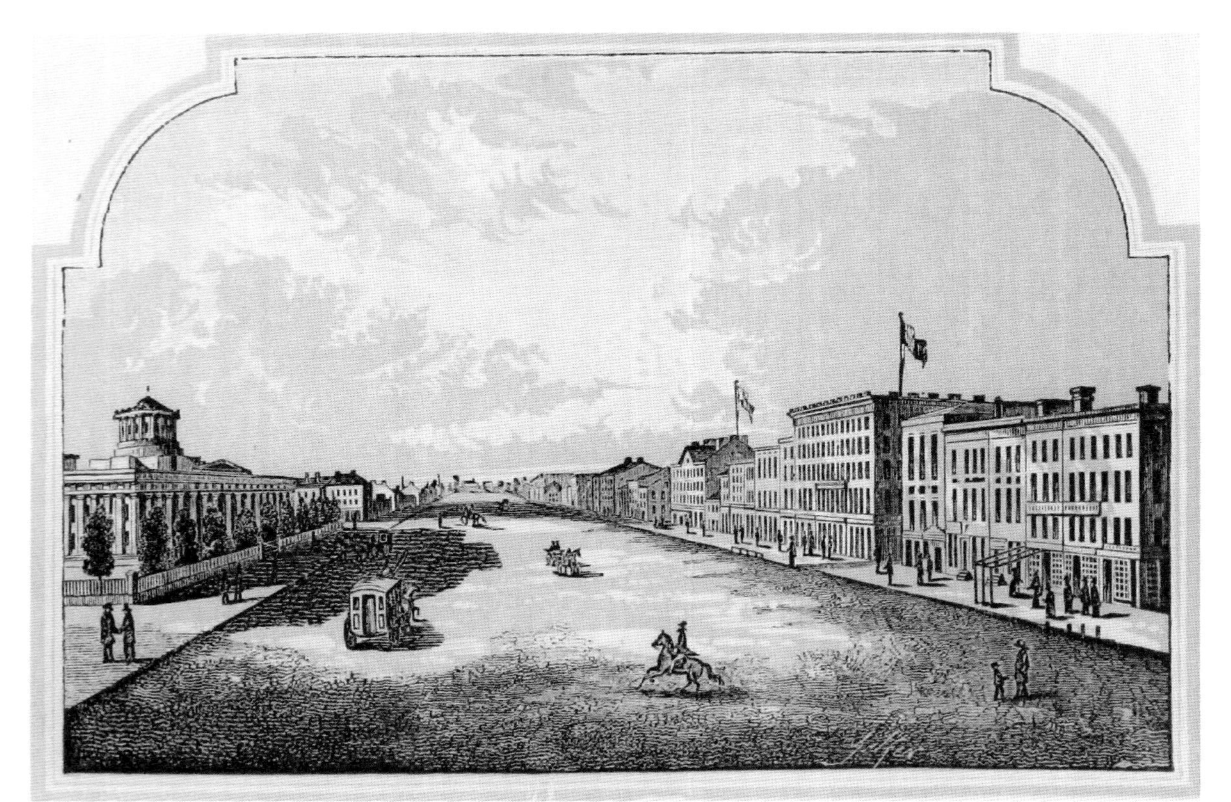

VIEW OF THE STATE HOUSE AND HIGH ST. COLUMBUS, O. FROM THE NORTH.

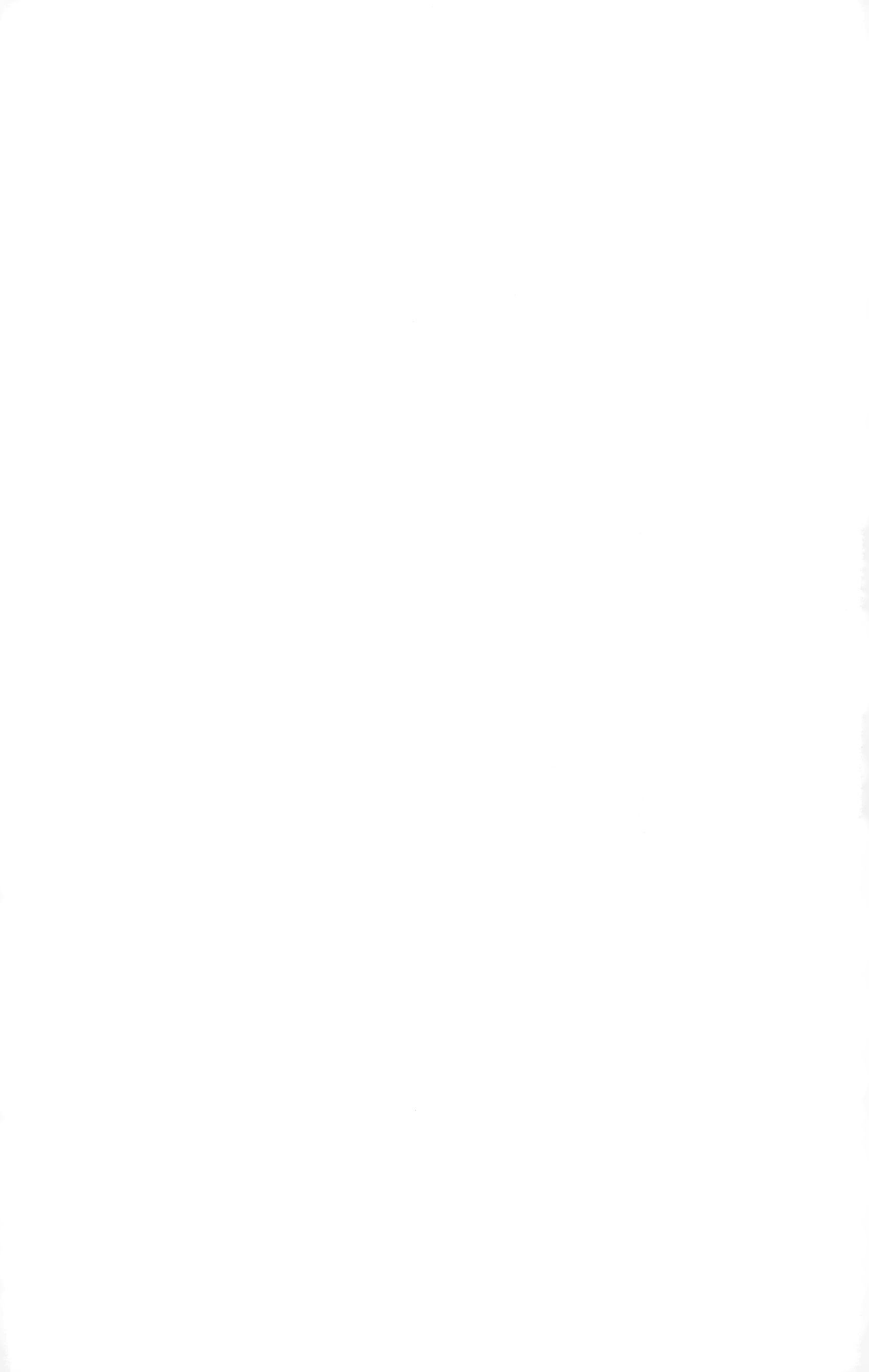

the party, when suddenly one of the warriors drew from beneath the skirts of his capote, a keen, bright tomahawk, walked rapidly up behind the chief, brandished it on high, and struck it into the head of his victim. Another blow, and Leatherlips was dead. The cold drops of sweat which were gathered on his neck and face, were pointed to, by his exultant executioners, as proofs of his guilt!

Such was an Indian execution, and all the circumstances about it prove how completely ignorance and superstition control the hearts of men, whether white, red, or black.

The seat of government, in Ohio, was not established till 1816. Prior to that, the sessions of the Legislature had been held at Chillicothe, and at Zanesville. In 1812, the proposals of Lyne Starling and others were accepted for the establishment of a permanent seat of government. The town was laid out in that year. On the 18th of June,—the same day on which war was declared with Great Britain,—the first public sale of lots was held. The first building erected for public worship, was built in 1814, for the Presbyterians. The first State House was built in 1814. The first session of the legislature held in Columbus, was in 1816. The first county Court House was built in 1819. The city charter was granted in 1834. Thus, though Columbus was laid out only forty years since in the woods, and had no mail for many years, yet it has grown up to be a large town. There are not more than thirty cities and towns in the United States, larger than Columbus. The progress of its growth has been thus:

In 1820, population	- - - -	1,400
In 1830 "	- - - -	2,437
In 1840 "	- - - -	6,048
In 1850 "	- - - -	17,100
In 1854 "	- - - -	22,000

The causes of its growth are various. The erection of many great public buildings; and the expenditure of large sums of public money, is one cause. Manufactories, of which there are several large establishments, is another. The great fertility of the surrounding country, adds also largely to its resources. The number of persons in public institutions and in public employment here, cannot be less than 1,000. At the present time, Columbus is likely to be the centre of numerous railways crossing the State in various directions.

The public buildings are so numerous and remarkable, as to be worthy of special note. Indeed, if the traveler can afford time to spend a day here, and examine the Lunatic Asylum, the Deaf and Dumb Asylum, the Blind Asylum, and the Penitentiary, he will be amply repaid for his trouble.

THE CAPITOL of Ohio, now near completion, is one of the largest, and most beautiful public buildings in the United States. It is built of Ohio marble, (as it is called,) which is a light gray limestone, at once durable and handsome. It is the largest building of the kind in the country, except the Capitol of the United States, at Washington. The following are the dimensions of some of the State Capitols, as reported by the State House Commissioners:

The Capitol of Ohio, at Columbus, is 304 by 184 feet, and covers an area of -	55,936	feet.
The Capitol of the U. S., at Washington, covers	61,693	"
The Capitol of Tennessee, at Nashville, is 240 by 135 feet, and covers - -	32,400	"
The Capitol at Raleigh, N. C. - -	14,940	"
The Capitol at Harrisburg, Penn. -	14,400	"
The Capitol of Indiana, at Indianapolis -	14,400	"
The Capitol of Vermont, at Montpelier -	12,200	"

It will be seen that the Capitol of Ohio is but slightly less in area than that of the United States; while it is nearly double the Capitol of Tennessee, and quadruple the largest in other states.

THE OHIO LUNATIC ASYLUM is a noble structure, occupying a commanding position, in an open space of ground about a mile east of the Capitol. There are thirty acres of ground attached to it, with a lawn in front, ornamented with shrubbery.

The building is in the form of a hollow square, the main front being 376 feet in length. The centre is 296 feet by 46 in depth. The wings 40 feet each, project beyond the centre 11 feet, and extend back 218 feet, thus forming a large court in the rear. The superficial fronts, (three sides,) of the building thus extend 812 feet. It contains 440 rooms, and covers an acre of ground. The style of the structure is in good taste, and it presents a very imposing appearance.

This institution commenced operations in November, 1838. From that time to 1851, there have been admitted 1,841 patients. Of these 897 have been cured.

Of the number of recent cases admitted to the Asylum, 75 per cent. recover, so that the chances of recovery from lunacy, when the patient is cared for in time, are very nearly as great as in any other disorder. Many are carried to the Asylum who have been hopelessly maniacs, or idiotic, for years, and therefore ought not to be included in the number from whom cures are expected.

THE OHIO PENITENTIARY, is also a very interesting institution. The building is an imposing edifice, on the east bank of the Scioto, just above the railroad bridge, and in sight of the cars. It is built of Ohio marble, and contains 350 cells in each wing. The cells are constructed of solid stone, with iron doors.

The Penitentiary generally contains about 500 prisoners, who are employed in useful manufactures, of various kinds. Many of them have been enga-

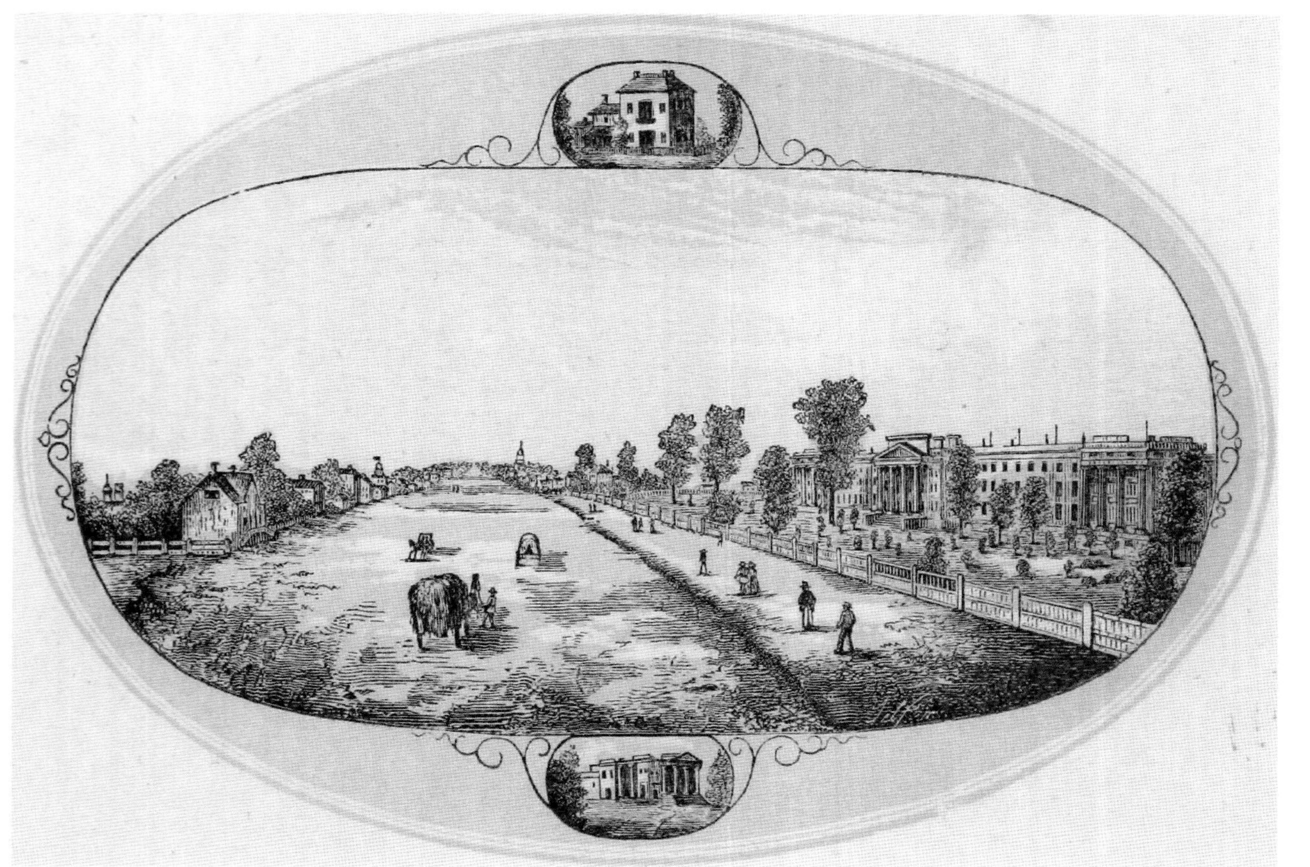

LUNATIC ASYLUM, COLUMBUS, O.

ged in the erection of the Capitol, in which they have done good service.

The labor of the prisoners yields about $20,000 per annum to the State; so that the cost of their support is not much. The discipline of the institution is very severe, and great effort is made to give the prisoners religious instruction. In some instances, no doubt, the instruction and discipline of the Penitentiary has proved useful, and there are those, who have come out reformed, and passed decent and respectable lives. But, on the whole, it is questionable whether penitentiary punishment is really beneficial. A large number of the prisoners learn more evil than good; and many come out more inveterate felons, than they went in; returning to the Penitentiary for new offences, two, three, and four times. Why can we not colonize our convicts in some Island of the Pacific? We should then remove the offending cause of crime, and put away so much evil from the community.

THE OHIO ASYLUM FOR THE DEAF AND DUMB, is also a well conducted and interesting institution. The building is built of brick, plain, with wings. In 1852 it contained 129 pupils. The instruction in the Deaf and Dumb Asylum has been very successful.

THE OHIO INSTITUTION FOR THE EDUCATION OF THE BLIND, was established in 1837, and like the other public institutions, is supported by the State. In 1852 the number of pupils was 68, and the instruction successful.

In addition to these public institutions, Columbus has a great many buildings of its own, and is, in fact, a very handsome town. The COUNTY COURT HOUSE is a handsome building. The NEIL HOUSE is one of the largest hotels in the United States. There are many and fine churches, with several private residences, of the most imposing appearance. Notwithstanding Columbus seemed to have no special advantages, as a town, it has nevertheless grown with great rapidity; and is now the third city of Ohio.

Columbus is also one of the railroad centres of the State. The Little Miami and Xenia R. R., on which we have been moving, here unites with the Cleveland, Columbus and Cincinnati R. R., making a continuous railroad line from Cincinnati to Cleveland, 252 miles in length.

THE COLUMBUS, PIQUA, AND INDIANA RAILROAD is between Columbus and Union, where it connects with the Indianapolis and Bellefontaine railroad; and thence to the Wabash and the Mississippi. It is 102 miles in length, and passes through Urbana and Piqua.

THE CENTRAL RAILROAD lies between Columbus and Wheeling, 140 miles. It passes through Newark and Zanesville; and is finished to Cambridge, 84 miles. The residue will be finished this year.

At Wheeling, the Central road will connect with the Baltimore and Ohio railroad, going to Baltimore, and with the Hempfield railroad, and thence to Philadelphia.

THE COLUMBUS AND CHILLICOTHE line is chartered and will be constructed.

From Columbus the traveler may proceed to all the most considerable towns in Ohio, and to all the cities of the Northern and Western States, by railway, reaching any of them in a very short time.

As a State Capital, Columbus will compare well with any of those in the older States. Of all the State Capitals, Columbus is the most populous, except Boston, Albany and Richmond; and in regard to public institutions and buildings, is thought to equal even them. When we reflect that it is only forty years since the town was laid out in a wilderness, this must be regarded as one of the most striking evidences of the rapid growth and prosperity of the Western people.

From Columbus, our route pursues the valley of the Olentangy, an Eastern branch of the Scioto. The railway company here is under a different charter—that of the Cleveland, Columbus and Cincinnati R. R. Co.,—but the whole line is worked together, and as to the public convenience and management, is, in reality, but one road.

From Columbus north, we still see the same fertile lands; but less cultivated than between Columbus and Cincinnati. The railway having been constructed but a few years, and departing, (on account of grades and distance,) widely from the public highways, does not pass through the old settled and cultivated lands. The traveler, therefore, will scarcely comprehend, without resorting to a book of statistics, how it is, that this portion of Ohio produces such an enormous quantity of grain, wool, and other valuable products. Without alarming you, my fellow traveler, with the dry bones of statistics, I may as well give you an idea of the production within an average of fifteen miles on each side of this road. Between Columbus and Cleveland, this road passes through some part of the following counties, viz: Franklin, Delaware, Morrow, Richland, Crawford, Huron, Lorain, and Cuyahoga. The general aggregate of agricultural productions in these counties, as ascertained by the last returns, was as follows: *two million eight hundred thousand bushels of wheat; five million eight hundred bushels of corn; six million seven hundred thousand pounds of butter; one million three hundred and sixty thousand pounds of cheese; and one million four hundred thousand pounds of wool.* This is a very great production for a surface of land not exceeding

DELAWARE STATION.

three thousand square miles. More than half of this production is *surplus*, which is carried to New England, and New York, chiefly for consumption. These facts show, that while there is no great display of farms on the immediate line of the road, there is within its reach a very fine agricultural section.

WORTHINGTON, 9 miles from Columbus, is the first considerable town we come to, north of Columbus. It is in sight, and not more than a half a mile from the road. Here the venerable Bishop CHASE commenced his labors in the west, in the service of religion and education; and from the station we may see the buildings where KENYON COLLEGE had its birth. Worthington derives its name from THOMAS WORTHINGTON, one of the earliest settlers, and most distinguished men in the State. He emigrated to Ohio about 1793, from Berkeley county, Virginia. Being extremely averse to slavery, he emancipated his slaves; but most of them desired to go with him; so that he brought about sixty of those emancipated slaves to this State. Their descendants make up a large part of the colored people at Chillicothe, where he resided. He was an active and most energetic man of business; but was very soon carried into public life, which henceforth occupied most of his time. He was a member from Ross county of the Convention which framed the first Constitution. He was one of the two first United States Senators from this State. He was ten years in the Senate, where he was of great service, in the business of the nation, and much confided in by the administrations of Jefferson and Madison. Subsequently, he was four years Governor of the State; and in his latter days Canal Commissioner. In all his public career, he rendered most useful service, and commanded universal respect.

DELAWARE, 24 miles from Columbus, is the county seat of Delaware county. It is about two miles from the main line, but has a side curve about five miles in length. Delaware was named by the Delaware Indians, one of the principal original tribes in the United States. The name of this once powerful tribe, says Col. John Johnston, is *Wa be nugh ka*, the people from the East, or sunrising. The tradition among themselves is, that at some remote period, they emigrated from the West, crossed the Mississippi, ascended the Ohio, and fought their way, till they reached the Delaware river, (named from Lord Delaware,) near where Philadelphia now stands, in which region of country they became fixed. They ever regarded the Quakers with respect and affection. They finally removed to the West, and some of them are now in the Indian Territory, west of the Mississippi.

Delaware was laid out by Moses Byxbe and the late Judge Henry Baldwin of Pittsburgh. The first brick house was erected in 1808, and there being no mason, Byxbe's *wife* laid all the brick on the inside walls. In the early settlement of the West, women had many employments which are now unknown to them—and there was little occasion for Women Rights' Conventions, when woman shared in all the labors, dangers, and glory of the pioneers.

It was not till 1823, that the first church was built; but now, Delaware is a large and flourishing village. By the census, Delaware town has 2,074 inhabitants. It has several churches, a large hotel, a bank, two newspapers, and all the other circumstantials which belong to a pleasant, growing town. Among the notables of the town, are Delaware Springs, and the Wesleyan University. The springs are said to be salutary, being strongly impregnated with sulphur and other mineral substances. The Wesleyan University was founded by the Methodists, and numbers the present year 594 students.

A BEAR FIGHT is very often talked about, but very seldom experienced. One occurred in this neighborhood, which is more remarkable than any I ever heard of. There was a Captain John Minter, among the early settlers, who was originally from Kentucky, and became famous by his great bear fight. Seeing a very large bear, he fired upon him, and the bear fell. Supposing him dead,—after reloading—he touched bruin's nose with his gun, when he instantly sprung up. He fired upon him again, only slightly wounding him. As the bear sprang forward, he threw his tomahawk at him, and finally broke his rifle on his head. All would not do: on came the enraged bear. Too late to escape, he drew his big knife, and made a plunge; but the beast struck it from his hand, and at once folded Minter in his embrace. Fortunately, he was tall, strong-muscled and athletic. The bear calculated upon hugging his adversary to death very soon; but Minter contrived to twist his body in such ways, that Mr. Bruin could not crush him. The woods were open, without underbrush, and they rolled over in every direction. Several times, he thought he was gone; but being strong, he choked the bear, when the latter would be obliged to let go a moment to knock off his hands. They struggled in this way for hours, when luckily, they rolled back near where the knife lay, when, after many efforts, he brought bruin near enough to grasp the knife. Then you may depend, he was not long in using it. He stabbed the bear repeatedly till he bled to death—never releasing his hold till life was gone! Not a rag was left on Minter; and his body and limbs were lacerated with the claws of the bear. He was only able to crawl to a log, till rested; and then could only crawl home, with no covering but blood. When his friends came to view the ground next morning, they found the surface torn up for half an acre. His scars and welts always remained—and he gave up hunting forever.

ASHLEY, 150 miles from Cincinnati, and 104 from Cleveland, is a small, new place, in Morrow county. This and the next five places, have wholly grown up since the location of the railroad.

CARDINGTON, 156 miles from Cincinnati, and 96 miles from Cleveland, is another new village of Morrow county. It contains about 400 inhabitants, and from all appearances, is growing with rapidity.

GILEAD STATION, 161 miles from Cincinnati, 41 miles from Columbus, and 91 from Cleveland. The village is about 2½ miles to the east. Gilead is the county seat of Morrow, and contains about 800 inhabitants. It formerly belonged to Marion county, from which it was set off, to make the new county

GALION, 174 miles from Cincinnati, and 78 from Cleveland. This is chiefly distinguished as a railroad station, and the intersection of the Cincinnati and Cleveland Railroad, with the Bellefontaine and Indiana Railroad. The Bellefontaine and Indiana is 118 miles in length, and at Union, the State line of Ohio and Indiana, connects with the Indianapolis and Bellefontaine Railroad, 83 miles in length, which make 201 miles from Galion to Indianapolis. There it connects with the various railroads going to Madison, Terre Haute, and La Fayette.

Galion is in the county of Crawford,—one corner of which we pass through.

Crawford county was named from Col. William Crawford, who also gave name to CRAWFORD'S DEFEAT, one of the most disastrous battles which ever took place between the whites and Indians. Crawford was a Virginian, born in the same year with Washington—who was his friend, and often, in his visits to the west, became an inmate of his humble dwelling, in Fayette county, Pennsylvania. He raised a regiment in the Revolution, by his own exertions, and became a Colonel of Continentals. In 1783, he very reluctantly engaged in this expedition against the Indians, the result of which was total defeat, and his own death, amidst excruciating tortures.

Whatever might have been Crawford's merits, the result was a measure of just retribution. In the preceding year, the whites attacked and destroyed the innocent and unoffending Christian Indians, at the Moravian Towns. The leader of this most cruel and horrid outrage, was a Col. Williamson. The poor Indians, unsuspicious, had quietly surrendered to Williamson and his men; who decided they should all be killed,—*murdered*. Their faith and devotion never left them; but they died amidst their prayers. "Their orisons were already ascending the throne of the Most High! The sound of the Christian hymn, and the Christian prayer, found an echo in the surrounding woods, but no responsive feeling in the bosom of their executioners. With gun, and spear, and tomahawk, and scalping knife, the work of death progressed in these slaughter houses, till not a sigh or moan was heard, to proclaim the existence of human life within. All died, save two Indian boys, who escaped, as if by miracle, to be witnesses in after times, of the savage cruelty of the white man towards their unfortunate race." Congress felt the atrocity of this act, and passed an ordinance for the encouragement of the Moravian Missions. Providence, however, avenged this murder in the most signal manner, as if purposely to mark the divine displeasure on the persecutors of his servants.

As we have said, in the year following, Col. Crawford reluctantly led a large body of frontier men, in another expedition against the Indians. Let it not be supposed, that any sentiment of mercy or humanity had entered the hearts of this body, in consequence of the preceding atrocities. On the contrary, this expedition was planned to destroy the Wyandot towns, on the Sandusky; and it was resolved to spare neither man, woman, or child—friendly or unfriendly. The intention of the whites was to proceed with secrecy; but this was vain. The Indians—by their scouts—knew their numbers, object, and plan. The army reached the upper Moravian towns; but they were deserted. It pursued its way across the Sandusky plains, till the Indians were met in full force. A battle ensued, in which neither party had the victory; but the Indians continued to increase in such numbers, that a retreat took place at night. In the retreat, several large parties detached themselves from the main body, thinking thus to avoid the Indians; but it turned out the reverse. These parties were nearly all cut off and destroyed. Col. Crawford, who had lingered behind, to look for, and save some of his friends, was cut off, and taken by the Indians. He was carried to the Indian towns, and after many tortures and cruelties, was burnt alive.

The danger of being found in *bad company*, was never more signally illustrated, than in this instance. Williamson, it was, as I have related, who had commanded the party, which destroyed the Moravian towns. The Indians looked upon him, as not only a cruel, but a very bad man, and were determined to have full vengeance. When Crawford took command of the second party, they associated him with Williamson—although they knew and had a good opinion of him. This association with Williamson, was the cause of his cruel death; for when Crawford sent for Wingemunn, a chief whom he knew, and who was friendly to him, Wingemunn told him that nothing could be done to save him; for he was in company with that bad man, Williamson. Crawford answered, that he went out to restrain Williamson, and prevent him from committing cruelties. Wingemunn replied, that the Indians would not believe that, if he told them; for they knew he could not prevent them.

A paragraph from this dialogue, as reported by Heckewelder, is worth quoting; for it shows the Indian sagacity and sense of justice. It is given thus:

Crawford—Out of my power! Have any Moravian Indians been killed or hurt since we came out?

Wingemunn—None; but you first went to their town, and finding it deserted, you turned on the path towards us. If you had been in search of warriors only, you would not have gone thither. Our spies watched you closely. They saw you while you were embodying yourselves on the other side of the Ohio. They saw you cross the river. They saw where you encamped for the night. They saw you turn off from the path to the deserted American town. They knew you were going out of the way Your steps were constantly watched, and you were suffered quietly to proceed, until you reached the spot where you were attacked."

Crawford felt that with this sentence, ended his last ray of hope, and now asked with emotion, "what do they intend to do with me?"

Wingemunn.—I tell you with grief. As Williamson and his whole cowardly host, ran off in the night, at the whistling of our warriors' balls, being satisfied that now he had no Moravians to deal with, but men who could fight, and with such he did not wish to have anything to do. I say, as they have escaped, and taken you, they will take revenge on you, in his stead."

And so they did. And the story of Crawford's defeat will long be remembered, for its woes and its losses. But was it not retributive justice? Was ever anything more cruel, more awfully unjust, than the slaughter of the peaceful, unoffending Moravian Indians? Was there ever a greater iniquity, than that act, as described by Wingemunn, of turning off from their real enemies, to pursue a second time, these poor Moravians?

I have given the story, as an illustration of our border wars, and of the frequent instances in which the whites were the aggressors. I have already said, that in fact, and ultimately, the barbarous Indians could have no solid right to a continent which they were unable to cultivate or civilize. That is true; but, atrocities such as that upon the Moravian Indians, can have no apology in any human code of morals. It was a dark wrong—diabolical in its spirit, and inhuman in its act.

CRESTLINE is an important railway station, at the intersection of two great lines of railway, viz: the Cincinnati and Cleveland line, and the continuation of the Pennsylvania Central, through Ohio and Indiana. From Crestline to Pittsburgh, by the Ohio and Pennsylvania Railroad, is 187 miles; and from Crestline to Fort Wayne, Indiana, 120 miles. From Pittsburgh to Philadelphia, is 353 miles. Thus, there is a continuous line of Railway, from Philadelphia,—*via* Pittsburgh, Crestline, Bucyrus, Crawford county, Lima, Allen county,—to Fort Wayne; thence, a system of railways—now constructing—will take the traveler to any point on the Ohio, the Wabash, or Lake Michigan. At Crestline, therefore, he can, if he please, depart to any point in the United States. Large and handsome depots and shops are erected here for the accommodation of the extensive business which must necessarily be conducted at this point.

SHELBY (of which we have given a view), is also an important station. Here the track of the Mansfield and Lake Erie Railroad, crosses that of the Cleveland and Cincinnati line. Here the traveler may have a choice of routes. He may go to Sandusky City, by the Mansfield Railroad, or he may go south to Mansfield, Mount Vernon, Newark, and Zanesville. At Newark, the Mansfield Railroad connects with the Scioto and Hocking Railroad, which will continue it to Portsmouth, on the Ohio. When completed, this will make one of the through lines of the State,—passing from Sandusky City, through Shelby, Mansfield, Mount Vernon, Newark, Lancaster, Logan, Jackson, to Portsmouth—and penetrating the western edge of the mineral regions of Ohio.

MANSFIELD,—for which Shelby is the station—is a large town of about 4,000 inhabitants—county seat of Richland county. It was named from General Jared Mansfield, Surveyor General of the Northwestern Territory, from 1803 to 1812. Richland is one of the great wheat counties, which extend in a sort of belt through this part of Ohio. It is quite singular, that although we are now in the most productive grain region of the United States, we see scarcely any indications of it! Everything is new, and the fields are not remarkably well cultivated. The reason, however, is obvious. The railway, to obtain proper grades, has gone on a new path, avoiding all the old highways, and therefore leaving out of sight, the best houses and farms. That we may have some idea, however, of what this wheat belt really does produce, I take the following facts from the Auditor of State's Report. Including the county we are in, there are just thirteen counties, viz: Morrow, Richland, Knox, Ashland, Wayne, Holmes, Coshocton, Stark, Tuscarawas, Columbiana, Carroll, Harrison, and Jefferson, between the west line of Richland and the Ohio River. These counties cover a surface of 6,000 square miles, and pro-

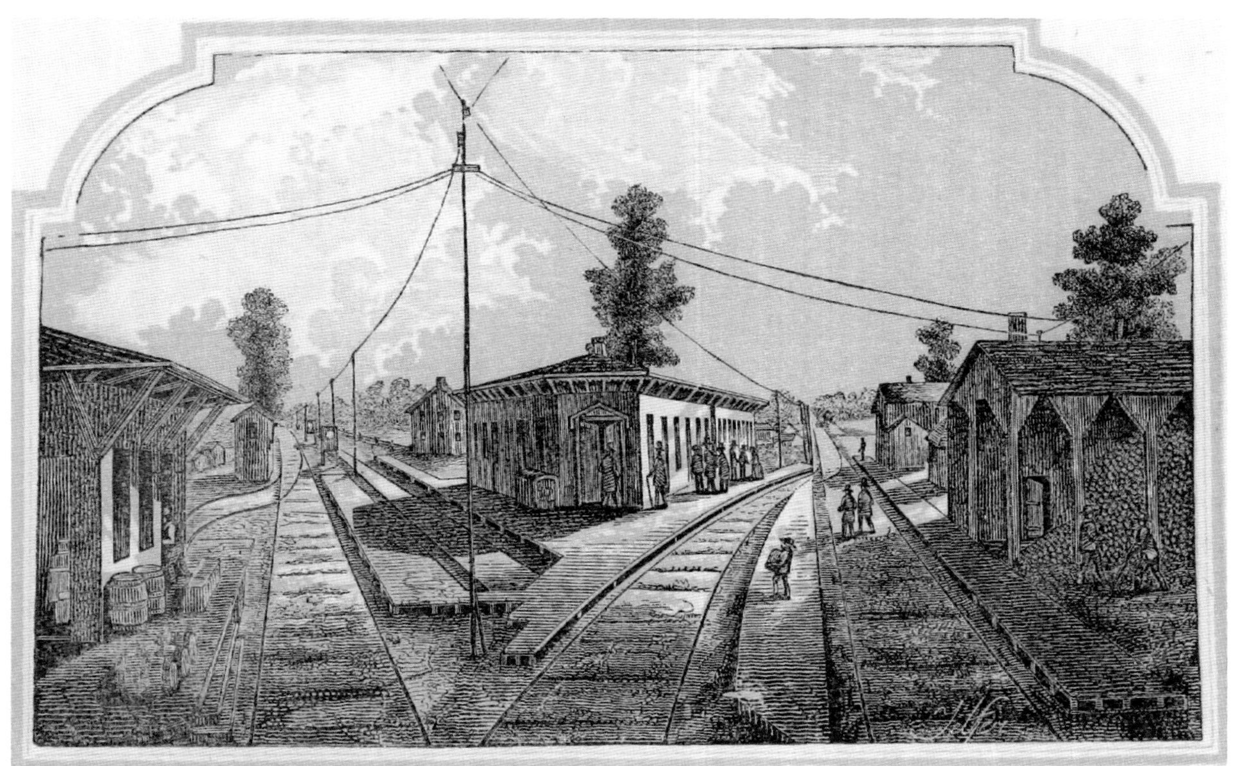

SHELBY JUNCTION.

duced in the year 1850, *nine million* of bushels of wheat, and *six million five hundred thousand* bushels of corn! These counties contained 350,000 inhabitants; so that they raised a *surplus* of at least six million of bushels of wheat! No part of the United States of equal extent, raises the same amount; indeed no single State produces a surplus equal to that of these counties, in 1850. If the traveler could leave the railway at the Shelby station, and take a buggy,—traveling on the common roads of the country,—he would then see something of these waving fields of wheat and corn, which make this the granary of the West.

SALEM is only a station, 193 miles from Cincinnati, and 60 miles from Cleveland. It is on the northern edge of Richland county.

GREENWICH, 199 miles from Cincinnati, and 54 miles from Cleveland, is in Huron, the western county of the Western Reserve.

The WESTERN RESERVE, as it is commonly called, is every where known as a particular section of Ohio—almost amounting to a separate State. It is also called "New Connecticut," from the fact that it was originally owned and chiefly settled by Connecticut. The manner in which it came to belong to Connecticut is very curious When the first charters were granted to the American Colonies, there was great ignorance in regard to the geography of this continent. Indeed, it was an unexplored region—a complete *terra incognita.* The charters, therefore, frequently conflicted with one another. This was the case with the charter of Connecticut, by which King Charles the II. conveyed to the Connecticut Colony, all the lands between the 41st and 42d degrees of latitude, from the Providence plantation to the Pacific Ocean! This, of course, conflicted with New York and Pennsylvania, with whom there immediately arose an altercation. In 1786, Connecticut, in common with the other States, granted to the General Government, all her western lands; but kept up her claims on Pennsylvania and New York. At length, the United States Government compromised the matter, by *reserving* to the State of Connecticut this district, containing 3,800,000 acres,—which the State has since sold, and the proceeds of which constitutes the basis of the Connecticut School Funds. The RESERVE contains twelve counties, viz: Ashtabula, Trumbull, Mahoning, Lake, Geauga, Portage, Cuyahoga, Summit, Medina, Lorain, Erie, and Huron. We are now traversing Huron. This is a productive county—being level and generally rich. The arable ground, (about 50,000 acres in cultivation), is about equally divided, between the culture of corn and wheat. Large parts of the lands of this county, however, are used as pastures and meadows—which feed great numbers of cattle and sheep.

Huron was originally constituted entirely out of the "Fire Lands,"—a body of land given by the State of Connecticut, to those of its citizens who suffered by fire in the revolutionary war. These were principally in the towns of Norwalk, Danbury, and New Haven. As usual, however, most of them fell into the hands of speculators, and some of them have been held by the original purchasers to this day.

We cross, near Greenwich, the head waters of Vermillion River, which empties into Lake Erie, at the port of Vermillion,—a place which has considerable commerce.

NEW LONDON is the next station, 47 miles from Cleveland. After leaving this station, we soon pass out of Huron county, and come to

ROCHESTER, 41 miles from Cleveland. This station is in Lorain county. This county has no great commercial town, but is nevertheless, a fast growing and flourishing district. It is much less productive in grain, than the counties we have just passed through, but has large numbers of cattle and sheep, and fine pasturage. Its principal towns are Elyria, the county seat, and the celebrated Oberlin. It is watered by Black River,—at whose mouth there centres considerable commerce. The rivers of the Reserve are all quite short—only about 40 or 50 miles in length—and not navigable—yet as their mouths constitute almost the only harbors on the Lakes, they have created points of concentration for navigation and commerce. This is the case with the Maumee, Sandusky, Huron, Vermillion, Black River, Cuyahoga, and Grand River; from all of which—even the smallest—there is a large export trade.

In traveling through Lorain and Cuyahoga, the traveler will note that he is not only in the "Reserve," but he is in a very different country, as to soil and geological appearances. In the Miami country, we found valleys of rich black soil, of exceeding fertility—surrounded by rolling hills, round and graceful. As we came through the wheat belt, we found the land rolling—but scarcely any hills—with a loamy soil,—neither the black alluvian, nor the clay; but well adapted to the small grain; but now, as we approach the Lake, the ground is flat and clayey—producing fine grass, but not very productive in grain. The original opinion held of these soils, may be known, by the early classification of soils. That of the Miami valleys, was set down as *first rate;* that of the middle counties, as *second rate;* and that of the Reserve, as *third rate.* Judged by the standard of Indian corn, this was a correct classification. But Nature has a way peculiar to every kind of soil, as well as plant. These lands of the Reserve, produce excellent grass; and its inhabitants make up in cheese, and butter, and wool, what they lack in corn.

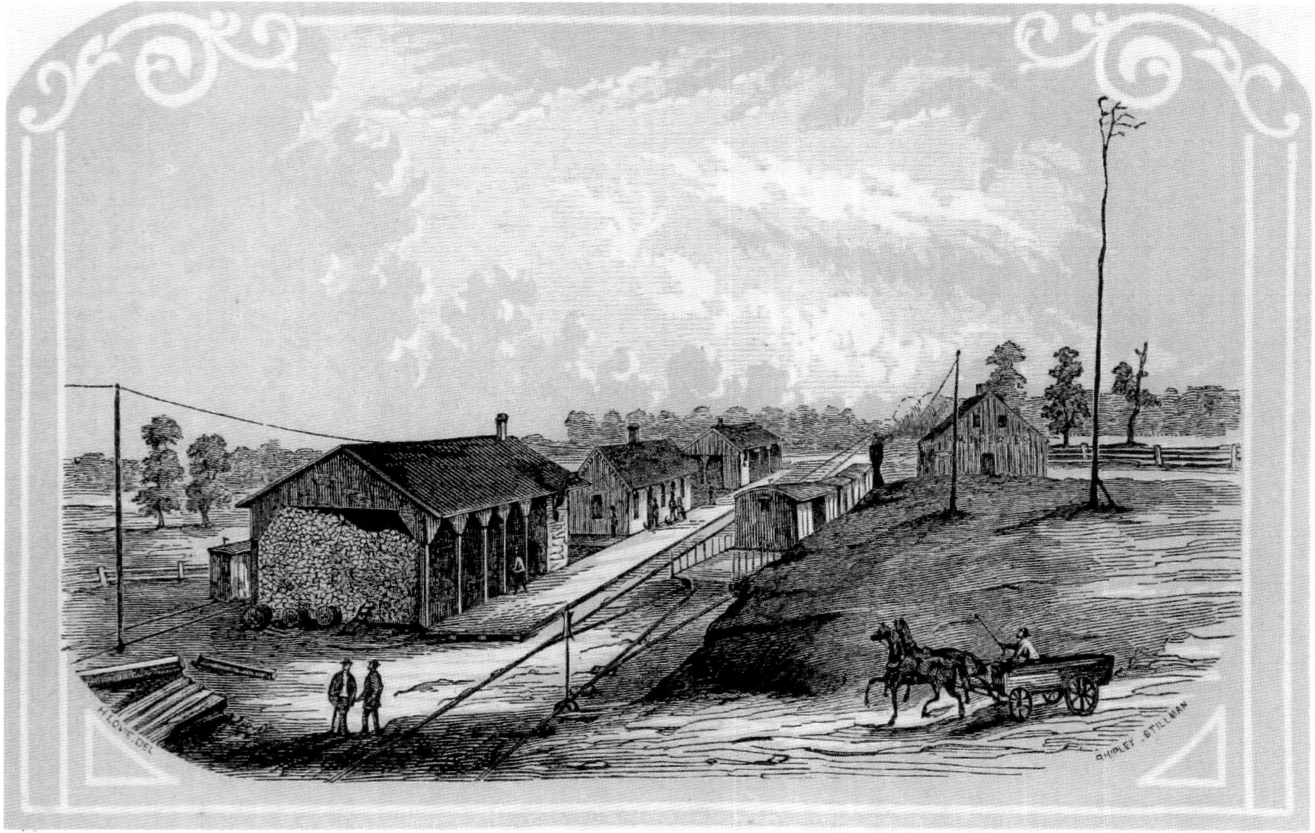

GRAFTON STATION.

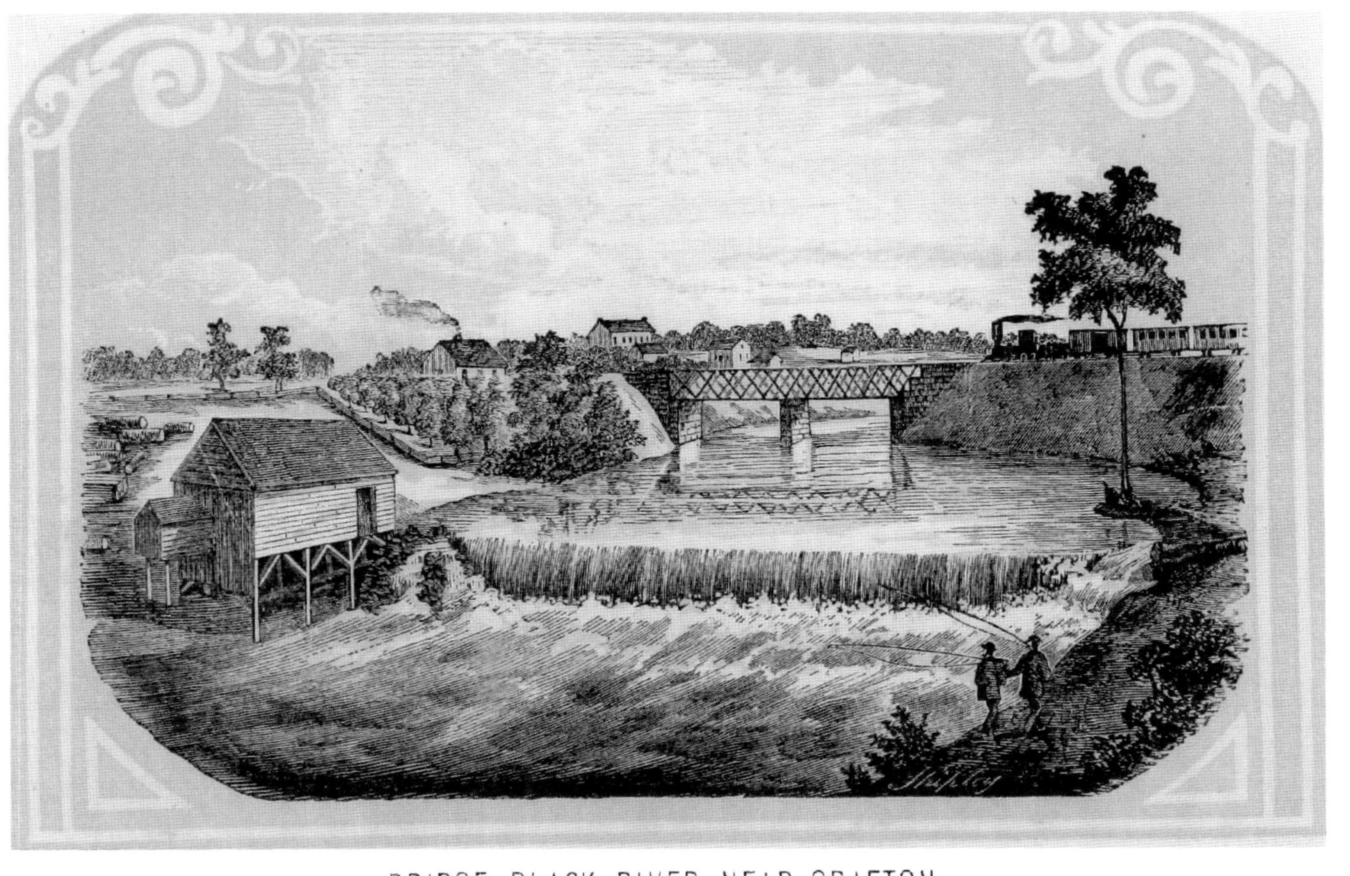

BRIDGE, BLACK RIVER NEAR GRAFTON.

WELLINGTON STATION, also in Lorain, is 36 miles from Cleveland. We are now about nine miles from OBERLIN, an institution, which, in its early stages, excited many prejudices; but which seems to have triumphed over all, and established for itself a high reputation. Its characteristics are peculiar. It is exclusively religious. It admits persons of both sexes, and all colors. It teaches the dead languages, but without the heathen classics; and it endeavors to give a thoroughly useful education—physical, moral, and intellectual. From 1840 to 1845, it had an average of 500 students annually; and we are informed it now has 1000. This is certainly great success as to numbers; and time seems to strengthen, rather than impair confidence in its usefulness.

LA GRANGE STATION is 29 miles from Cleveland.

GRAFTON, 25 miles from Cleveland, is at the intersection of the Cleveland and Columbus Railroad with the Toledo, Norwalk, and Cleveland Railroad, and also at the crossing of Black River. The Toledo, Norwalk, and Cleveland Railroad, commences at Toledo, where it connects with the Michigan roads, and passing through Fremont, the county seat of Sandusky, and Norwalk, the county seat of Huron, intersects the Cleveland road, at this place. From Grafton to Toledo is 84 miles; and from Cleveland to Toledo is 112 miles, which is run in about five hours. On the opposite page, is a view of Grafton station.

OLMSTEAD, 15 miles from Cleveland. Near this, we cross Rocky River, by a fine bridge.

Here, we begin to see a few scattered pines and cedars—denoting a total change in the geological features of the country. From this to Western New York, and Northern Pennsylvania—comprehending a very large tract of country—the pine is one of the predominant trees—diversifying the scenery with its deep evergreen and its straight trunk.

BEREA is three miles further, at the falls of the east branch of Rocky River. Berea is chiefly known for its grindstones, of which there are great numbers made here. It was originally laid out by a sort of stock company, who had formed high ideas of the benefits of association.

At this point, we are very near the Junction Ohio Railroad, from Cleveland to Sandusky—which, however, pursues a separate track to Cleveland. This road is now consolidated with the Toledo, Norwalk, and Cleveland—under the name of the CLEVELAND AND TOLEDO Railroad, whose President is the Hon. Samuel F. Vinton.

ROCKPORT, 7 miles from Cleveland, is the next station. We are now gradually descending the slope from the great plain of Ohio to the Lake. We approach Cleveland through a deep ravine, into the

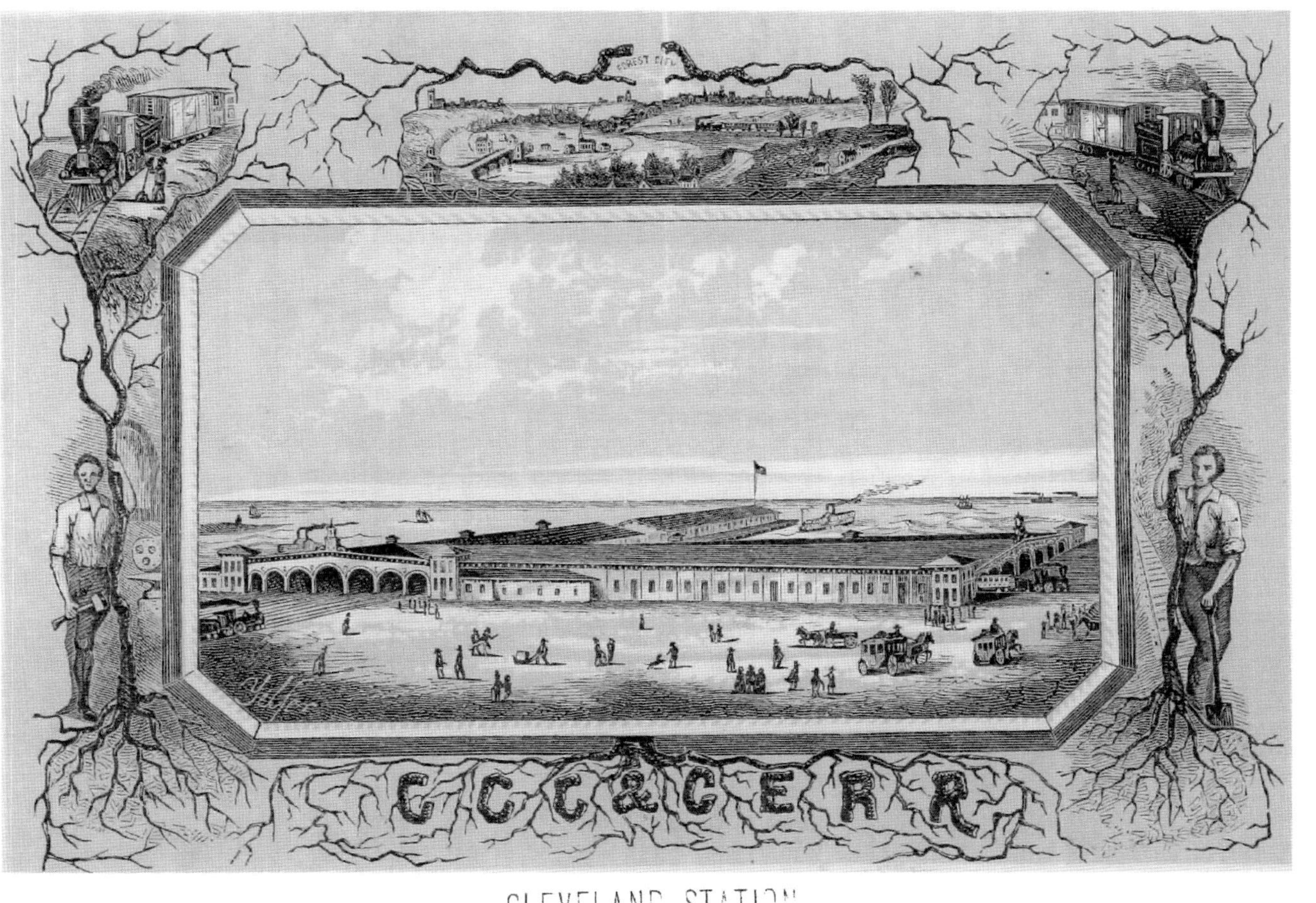

CLEVELAND STATION

valley of the Cuyahoga, and find our depot nearly down to the level of the Lake—and in the midst of the shipping and bustle of what seems to be a seaport.

Accompanying this, is a plate of the Depot Buildings, Pier, and Harbor of Cleveland. The depot here is a very bustling place—crowded with multitudes of cars, and draymen, hackmen, porters, steamboat runners, &c., innumerable. Let the traveler take care of himself; for, although the railways and their officers and agents, are all systematic and orderly; yet in such a crowd there is abundant need of the caution which we see posted up, "BEWARE OF PICKPOCKETS."

CLEVELAND, 253 miles from Cincinnati, and (*via* the Erie Railroad,) 602 miles from New York, is called the Forest City—and most appropriately, too; for nearly all the streets are shaded with beautiful trees. Cleveland is the second town in Ohio, and one of the most flourishing in the United States. Including Ohio City, its growth has been thus, viz:

In 1825,	500
In 1830,	1,000
In 1835,	5,000
In 1840,	6,071
In 1845,	12,000
In 1850,	22,000
In 1854, (estimated)	37,000

Including Ohio City—separated only by the Cuyahoga—and with which it is now united—it is the *twenty-second* town in magnitude in the United States. It was founded by General MOSES CLEVELAND, in 1796, and named after him. For nearly thirty years, till 1825—when the canal got into full operation—Cleveland was only a small, straggling village—beset with sickness, and consequently a bad name. In the uncultivated state of the country—and while the banks of the Cuyahoga were yet overhung with decaying vegetation—fevers infected the inhabitants, and the place was shunned by the immigrant. When the Ohio canal was completed, the business temptations to settle at Cleveland, were too great to be resisted. Vegetation became less luxuriant, and gradually the town recovered from both the fact and the fame of fever. After 1830, (as the above figures show), the town rapidly grew. Its advantages for business are very great—being the outlet of the Ohio canal, and the best harbor on Lake Erie, within an hundred miles. The canal brought to it the vast export trade of Northern Ohio—especially of the great wheat counties, and for the same reason, it became an *entrepot* of imported goods. This gave it the first impulse. Then came the era of railways; and Cleveland was one of the first western towns to foresee and take advantage of the new system of commerce and locomotion. So

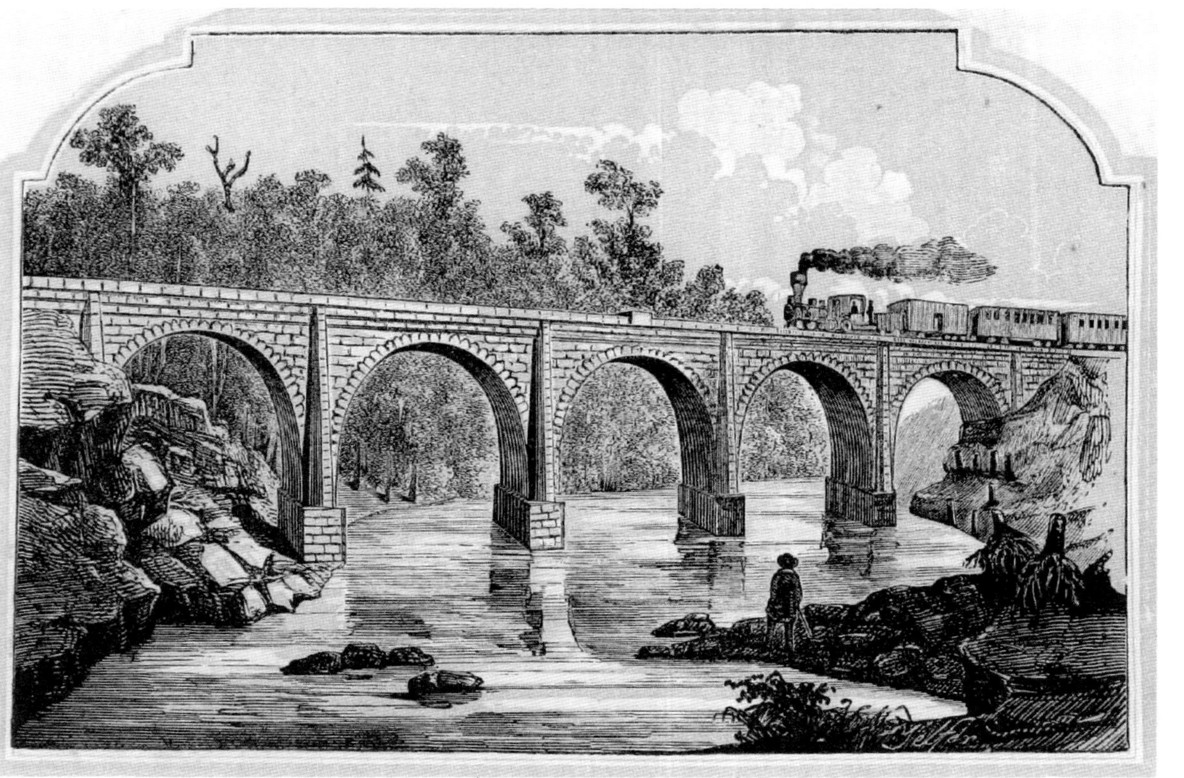

WEST BRANCH ROCKY RIVER, NEAR OLMSTEAD STATION.

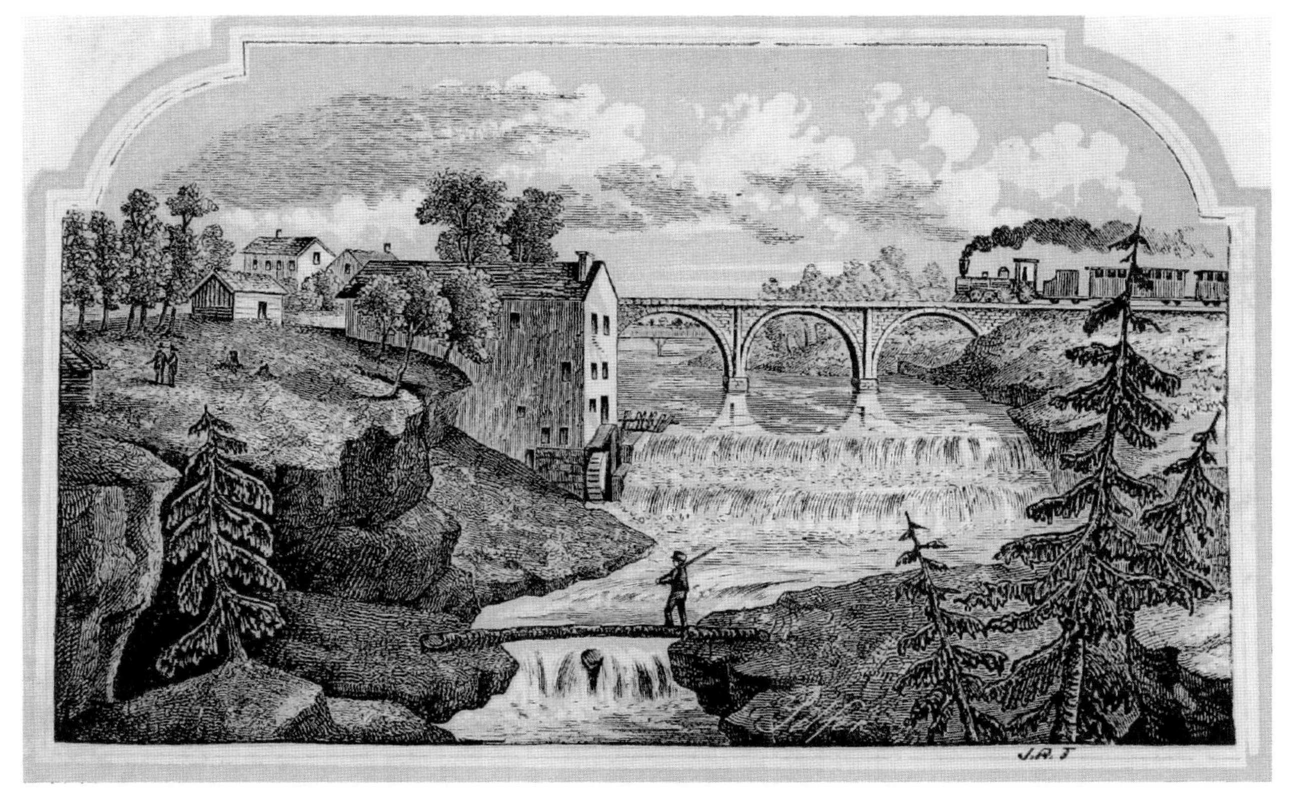

EAST BRANCH ROCKY RIVER, BEREA STATION.

it received a second great impulse, and is now growing with great rapidity. In 1860, it will, in all probability, have some 60 or 70,000 inhabitants, and will have surpassed all but some fifteen or sixteen cities of the United States.

In order to give some idea of its commercial importance, I annex some statistics of its exports and imports—which, dry as they are, may nevertheless interest the mercantile traveler. The reports of the Board of Public Works, in Ohio, enable us to see how much of strictly Ohio products *arrive* at this port; though even this will be incomplete; for of course much is brought by railway. The report gives the *arrival* of the following articles, at Cleveland, by canal, for 1853, viz:

Flour,	589,466	bbls.
Wheat,	1,817,677	bushels.
Pork,	12,198	bbls.
Whisky,	39,807	"
Bacon,	1,160,624	lbs.
Butter,	1,844,554	"
Cheese,	1,178,525	"
Wool,	1,200,903	"
Iron of all kinds,	9,700	tons.
Coal,	4,969,174	bushels.

These, with numerous other minor articles received and handled at Cleveland, of the produce of Ohio, make up *ten millions of dollars in value;* while the products of other States, and of foreign growth received here, amount to many millions more. There is room, therefore, for an extensive commerce—and as we look into the Harbor, we shall see steamers, schooners, propellers, canal boats, in every direction. Scarcely a moment passes, that there is not some sail vessel, or some smoking steamer arriving or departing. In fact, Cleveland has both the elements and the appearance of a commercial seaport; and one, which is yet in the very youth of its growth and vigor. All is activity and bustle. All is newness, freshness, and the springing elasticity of conscious strength.

Let us turn now to its RAILROADS, which are hereafter to constitute one of the main elements of its prosperity. We have now traveled 252 miles on the line from Cincinnati. This line was originally constructed by three companies—the Little Miami, the Xenia and Columbus, and the Cleveland, Cincincinnati and Columbus. The interests of the two former have been united; and now the whole line is run by two companies, meeting in Columbus. The railways at present concentrating in Cleveland, are

The Cleveland and Cincinnati Line,........ .	252	miles.
The Cleveland and Erie Line,.	95	"
The Cleveland and Toledo Line, (northern division,)	60	"
" " " (southern division,)	88	"
The Cleveland and Pittsburgh Line,... ..	99	"

The Cleveland and Zanesville Line,. ..	104 miles.
To Cleveland, proper,...	698 "

The last line is only completed in part; but the whole is in course of construction. By these several railways, connections are made between Cleveland, and almost every important point in the United States. The following are the principal railway routes, as formed by these connections, viz:

To New York, *via* Erie and Dunkirk,.... 602	miles.
To Cincinnati, ... .252	"
To St. Louis, *via* Toledo, Chicago, and Alton,.. .631	"
To Baltimore, *via* Pittsburgh,.. .. .. .492	"
To Philadelphia, *via* Pittsburgh and Harrisburgh. .480	"
To Washington City, *via* Baltimore,........ .516	"
To Boston, *via* Albany,. .. .. .684	"

From each of these cities, again, there are connections with all the principal interior towns; so that, from Cleveland the traveler may find his way, in a very short time, to any point his business or pleasure may lead him. Cincinnati may be reached in nine hours; Philadelphia, New York and Baltimore in 24 hours. How wonderfully everything has changed in a very few years! I remember when it took a week to go from Cleveland to Cincinnati, and that, too, a week of hard work!

The united effects of large commerce—of rapid and cheap locomotion—of a healthy, tonic air—of an industrious people, and a moral and religious tone of society, are the building up of Cleveland, not only in property, but in a beautiful and attractive form. If the traveler has time to walk about, and take a view of the upper town, he will find Cleveland one of the most charming places in this country. We have approached it—as railways always do large towns—in a most unattractive way, and looked only at the ravine and low valley of the Cuyahoga, with its untidy and unarchitectural buildings. But not so Cleveland on the hill. The broad and regular streets, shaded with lofty trees—the blocks of fine buildings—the neat private residences—the numerous churches, schools and seminaries—the large public square, with its walks and avenues—the glorious look-out on the Lake—all conspire to please and charm the stranger. The SCENERY of Cleveland is lovely; and yet it is without mountain, rock or torrent. It is the beautiful, without the sublime.

Here, in coming from the south, we first touch the shores of LAKE ERIE—and the first sight of it, if on a bright day, is a glorious sight. It is like, and yet not like, the Ocean. There are two things on the shore of the Ocean which always tell us it *is* the Ocean, and we do not find them on the Lake. One is the regular surge of the tides. Lake Erie has no tides; and one who has seen the Ocean, misses that regular heave and roar of the waters. Another is, the coast of the Sea has everywhere a certain primitive *hardness* of feature, which you do not see here. You find yourself on the shore of a great, broad water, which to the eye seems like the Ocean—a vast, sublime expanse of waters; but something reminds you it is not the Ocean, and you look around in a surprised and wondering delight. The surprise would be much greater if we were not well prepared beforehand, to meet such a view.

As a scene, the Lake has always something to interest you. Whether seen in a dark night, amidst scowling tempests and livid lightnings, or in the peaceful calm of a summer's day, it is always interesting. There is scarcely an hour in a clear day, in which several sail vessels may not be seen on its bosom. On the distant horizon, they seem like some light cloud floating on the water, while near by they loom up, under full canvass, glistening in the sun, and majestically approaching. Near by are the fiery steamers, sending forth their dark columns of smoke, and hurrying on with superhuman power. You look over the waters, and strain your eyes in vain to catch the Canada shore, which you know is there, but which seems now buried in the blue sky. You look in vain; but every now and then think you see the blue distant hills, when in fact they are only banks of clouds on the far horizon.

The LAKES of North America form, perhaps, the most remarkable feature of this continent. The

Caspian Sea, it is true, is larger than either one of them; but neither the Caspian, nor any collection of Lakes or Seas, is at all comparable to the chain of the American Lakes, which, extending from the Lake of the Woods to the Gulf of St. Lawrence, make, in fact, a continual succession of inland Seas, extending (Lake Michigan included) nearly 2000 miles in extent.

Lake Erie—the sixth in the series—is, in round numbers, about 240 miles in length, by 40 in breadth. This is not more than one-fourth the surface of Lakes Huron or Superior; but is in some particulars more interesting than either. Its commerce is now greater than that of either of the Lakes, and, at its eastern extremity, the whole body of its waters is poured over the rapids and falls of Niagara. The cause and phenomena of Niagara Falls are all explained by a simple reference to the comparative levels of Lakes Erie and Ontario. Lake Erie is 565 feet above tide water, and 322 feet above Lake Ontario. The consequence of this difference is, that the waters of Erie have to descend 565 feet to reach the Ocean, of which 322 feet are between Buffalo and Lake Ontario—only about 40 miles. Part of this is accomplished in the rapids above and below the Falls; but the great descent is at Niagara, where may be seen and studied, in all its glory, that wonderful phenomenon of nature, the FALLS OF LAKE ERIE—for such it is—

over the grand rock rampart which separates it from Ontario.

Has Lake Erie a tide? is a question which seems to have puzzled the natural philosophers, though now satisfactorily settled. A tide like the Ocean it was never supposed to have. But the Lake was observed to be higher in some years than in others. This was thought by some to be a regular rise and fall. Of late years, however, exact observations have been kept, and compared with those in former time; and the result is, that the rise and fall of the Lake is proved to be very irregular, and to depend merely upon the greater or less fall of water on the great northern plain, whose springs and rains mainly supply the Lakes. The descent of water is various, in different years, and cannot be carried off suddenly, because the obstruction at Niagara is uniform, and the waters of Erie must rise above the ordinary level before the amount carried over the rock ledge of Niagara will be sensibly increased. Col. WHITTLESEY of Cleveland, a distinguished geologist, has given the result of observations on the variations in Lake Erie; and it appears that the whole rise is only from 1½ to 3 feet, and it requires several months—sometimes much more time—for the water to ascend even that height. One important fact may be deduced from this: that there is no danger of overflow on the shores of the Lake, except from those sudden dashes made by a storm; and that is injurious only at the mouths of creeks and rivers, where the water accumulates. These mouths of streams, however, are harbors, generally protected by artificial works, as we see here at Cleveland, where the government has secured the entrance by two long stone piers.

FAREWELL to Cleveland! We may see it again, and often; but some of us will see it no more. What a miscellaneous company we are with in these cars! Some, no doubt, are familiar with this road, and will frequently pass here; but more are total strangers, and are going to distant regions, whence they will never return. And so we meet once in the brief journey of life, and look upon each other's faces, seen no more, till we shall meet at the general resurrection! We meet like ships at sea—crossing each other once on the broad ocean of time; thence borne by the winds to distant parts, or, may be in the deep waters buried; but borne quickly and forever from sight. We meet, like two little waves on yon broad Lake, to mingle once, then beat on the shore, and disappear forever!

Some meet, like two glad stars, rejoicing in their way, and parting with smiles. Some meet, like two dark clouds, made sad by the winds of sorrow, and parting in tears. But all part, never again to meet in the same assembly. Let us remember this, and do what we can to make the passing hours agreeable.

We are human—let us be humane. Even little things are of consequence in the aggregate of life; and the little service, the pleasant smile, the cheerful word, will all do good, and be remembered in the general account of good deeds performed on earth. But here we are. Where are we?

THE CLEVELAND AND ERIE RAILROAD is now before us. It is 95 miles in length, and is run by two companies—one from Cleveland to the Pennsylvania Line, and one from the Line to Erie. It is one of the pleasantest roads (at any rate in the day line), there is in the country. At first we follow the *shore* of the Lake, under the town, and leaving all its pretty streets, and fine houses, and picturesque scenery above us. But we have got the Lake before us, and that is a grand thing in itself. See yonder white sailed schooner—how gracefully she bends to the gentle wind, and looms above the water! She is like a very bird, and seems the Spirit of the Lake. What dark thing is that, as far off as you can see, almost? Ah! she is a steamer—a packet from Detroit, perhaps. These Lake steamers are noble vessels—and like our cars here, are filled up with human beings, going here and there, up and down upon the earth. What in this world takes so many people all over the country? What takes *you* and *me?* I, you see, am just here to watch you all, and put you down in a book. But what are *you* doing?

Going to buy goods? To see Niagara? To visit your old parents? To visit Babylon—that is, New York? To get married? To mourn, or rejoice, or what? What does take us all along from State to State, and town to town? I will venture to say you are all on a different errand—and some of you to very strange places. I once was going along this very place, and met a young man who seemed to be rather *high*, but then he talked straight, and he walked straight; but he looked wild—and he was talking about the New Jerusalem, and the Millenium, and Heaven. *He* was going to the Lunatic Asylum. I suppose he thought more of religion than the world in general—and the world being the majority, said he was insane.

Another time, there were two young men with handcuffs on, and they were going to the Penitentiary. Again I saw a man who was *high*, and he jumped off the cars—going 30 miles an hour—to get low; and when we left, he was *going down hill.* Then I saw a girl who had married at 15, with a baby at her breast—and she was *going to have a hard life.* Then I saw another, smiling and blushing—and she was *going to be married;* and at last, I saw one clothed in black, and tears upon her cheek. She was *going to a funeral* in the next village. Finally, I saw a slender man, whose cheeks were sunk, whose eye was glassy, whose heart heaved with a cough—and he was *going to the grave.* Then there were crowds of the gay and happy—all mingled in the passing throng; all parts of the great moving caravan of humanity—all hurrying along through their brief but varied hour.

"No more of this, if thou lov'st me, Hal," says some gay traveler, who would enjoy the passing hour; and he is right. The *present* is ours, and let us enjoy what we may, and learn what we can.

After a few miles, we leave the Lake shore, and getting on the general plain, pass through the interior—generally two or three miles from the Lake.

EUCLID, 10 miles from Cleveland, is the first station east. The village lies a mile or two from the station. The ownership of Euclid arose from a *strike* among the surveyor's men. They demanded higher wages; and General Cleveland, the agent, finally agreed to allow them a pre-emption of a township of land, at an agreed price. This settled the difficulty, and this is the way Euclid was purchased and settled. On the next page, is a view of the railway bridge over Euclid creek, with the village in the distance.

WICKLIFFE STATION, 4 miles from Euclid, 14 from Cleveland.

WILLOUGHBY, 19 miles from Cleveland, is at the crossing of Chagrin River, and in the county of Lake.

LAKE COUNTY was formed in 1840, from Geauga and Cuyahoga counties, and then contained 13,717 inhabitants. In 1850, it contained 14,654. Having no considerable town, except Painesville, and the lands being already occupied, its growth is slow. Yet its *density* of population—70 to a square mile—is greater than that of the State generally.

The village of Willoughby, (originally called Chagrin) is called from Professor Willoughby, of Herkimer county, New York. It is on Chagrin River, 2½ miles from its mouth. It is a neat and pleasant village—with several public buildings, built in the rural style.

Some 15 miles south of this town, is the flourishing and pretty village of CHAGRIN FALLS. In this township, there is a fall of 225 feet, in Chagrin River, which furnishes power for extensive machinery. It has a population of 1,250—with churches, schools, stores and factories.

Here, again, we are reminded how much of what *was* has disappeared to make room for what *is*. On the site of Chagrin was once an Indian town, and here were traces of their mounds and forts. Nor was this all. Here were large numbers of the elk, along this Lake. I do not know whether the buffalo were here—probably not, for they are accustomed to the prairies; but they were abundant in Ohio. So the red Indian, the elk, the buffalo, the bear, the

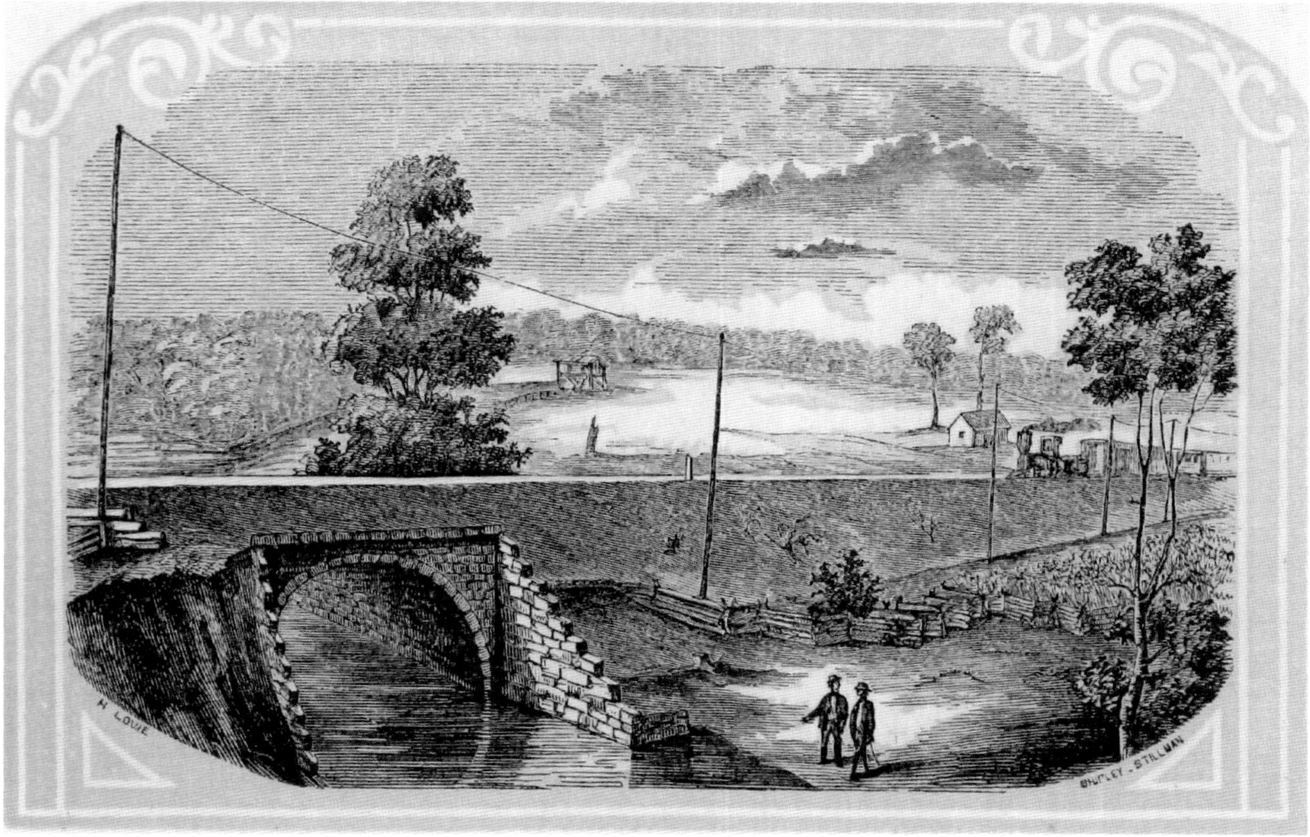

EUCLID CREEK.

ELK CREEK.

wolf, all of human or animal, which once inhabited this beautiful country, have disappeared. They are no more dwellers here, and their name, and character, and history, will be mysteries and antiquities to coming generations.

But a stranger people yet, one of whom you have heard, and will hear much, were here. At Willoughby we are about four miles from Kirtland city, and the Mormon Temple, which was the first establishment of the Mormons in the west. Who are the Mormons? The Mormons, you are aware, now inhabit Utah Territory, mostly dwelling near the Great Salt Lake. There they were driven by persecutions in Illinois and Missouri; persecutions, however, which were solely occasioned by their opposition to the accustomed laws, usages and religion of the country. They now have a territory to themselves, and have adopted and practiced the Asiatic custom of polygamy, contrary alike to the laws of God and to the laws of the United States. At present they dominate, unopposed, in the great waste territory of Utah; but how long they will be allowed to do so, is problematical.

The origin and progress of the Mormons make one of the most curious chapters in the whole history of delusion. The following facts seem to be authentically proved: The Mormons derive their name from the Book of Mormon, which they say was translated from gold plates, found in a hill near Palmyra, New York. But when and how written was this book of Mormon? About 1809–10. Solomon Spalding, then about 48 years of age, and who was born in Connecticut, removed to what is now Lake county, and amazed himself with writing a romance, called the "Manuscript Found." This undertook to show that the American Indians were descendants of the Jews—the lost tribes—and gave an historical account of them. This "Manuscript Found" was, after Spalding's death, traced to a printing office in Pittsburgh, but not printed. About 1823–4, *Sidney Rigdon*, one of the earliest preachers of Mormonism, came to Pittsburgh, ostensibly to *study the Bible.* Soon after, Rigdon commenced preaching some new doctrines, which were afterwards found to be in the book of Mormon. He was then acquainted with Jo. Smith, who was hunting gold mines in northern Pennsylvania. The Smith family then announced that a book had been discovered, which would give an account of the origin of the Indians. Rigdon had already prepared the minds of many persons for the reception of a new and miraculous book. When printed, the book was immediately carried to Rigdon, who pretended to disbelieve it—was then converted—repaired to Jo. Smith, and was appointed elder, priest, scribe and prophet. But what was this new book? Nothing else than Spalding's "Manuscript

Found"! John Spalding, Henry Lake, and six other witnesses, testify that the book of Mormon is the same, or nearly the same, with the "Manuscript Found," as read to them by Spalding. There is no doubt upon that subject. This manuscript, so innocently written, was thus fraudulently put forth to ignorant and credulous people, as a new revelation, and has ever since, and quite successfully, been preached as such. Its disciples call themselves the "Latter day Saints," and, with the exception of a few artful leaders, are probably as sincere as the believers in other doctrines. Most of them are a very ignorant people, and many come from Europe—from Manchester and Wales. We can readily see how such might easily be imposed upon; but the most remarkable thing about this imposture is, that some of its disciples are from the most intelligent parts of New England, and have received some education!

I recently saw in a newspaper the letter of a New England woman, who claims to be the wife of one Elder Pratt in Utah, to her sister in New Hampshire. She declines visiting her relatives, because there is such a difference in their usages and customs; for example, she is *one* of the seven wives of this Orson Pratt, who delights in *twenty-five children*, and is yet in middle life. She thinks it is a capital mode of life—the wives dwelling in sisterly love, and contributing to the comfort and happiness of this excellent man, who is improving on American manners and morals, by imitating the old patriarchs of Canaan and Chaldea.

In this state of things there arises a curious question. Are we to admit Utah as a State of the Union, in this heathenish condition? Or, when, as must be the case, other kinds of people come to settle in Utah, are they likely to suffer these abominations any more than they did in Missouri or Illinois? Very doubtful. Let time determine.

PAINESVILLE, 29 miles from Cleveland, is one of the principal towns of northern Ohio. It has several churches, stores, schools, printing office, bank, and near 2000 inhabitants. It was named from General EDWARD PAINE, an officer of the Revolution.

Painesville is the county seat of Lake county, and is one of the most beautiful villages of this part of Ohio. It lies on Grand River, which skirts the village on the east, in a deep and picturesque valley. The village is scattered, with cultivated gardens, ornamental trees and shrubbery. A public square, adorned with trees, contains the public buildings.

One of the early settlers of Painesville was SAMUEL HUNTINGTON, second Governor of the State, and a native of Connecticut. He was a man of high character, and one of the early pioneers of the Reserve. He originally settled at Cleveland, where he met with a singular adventure. This part of the

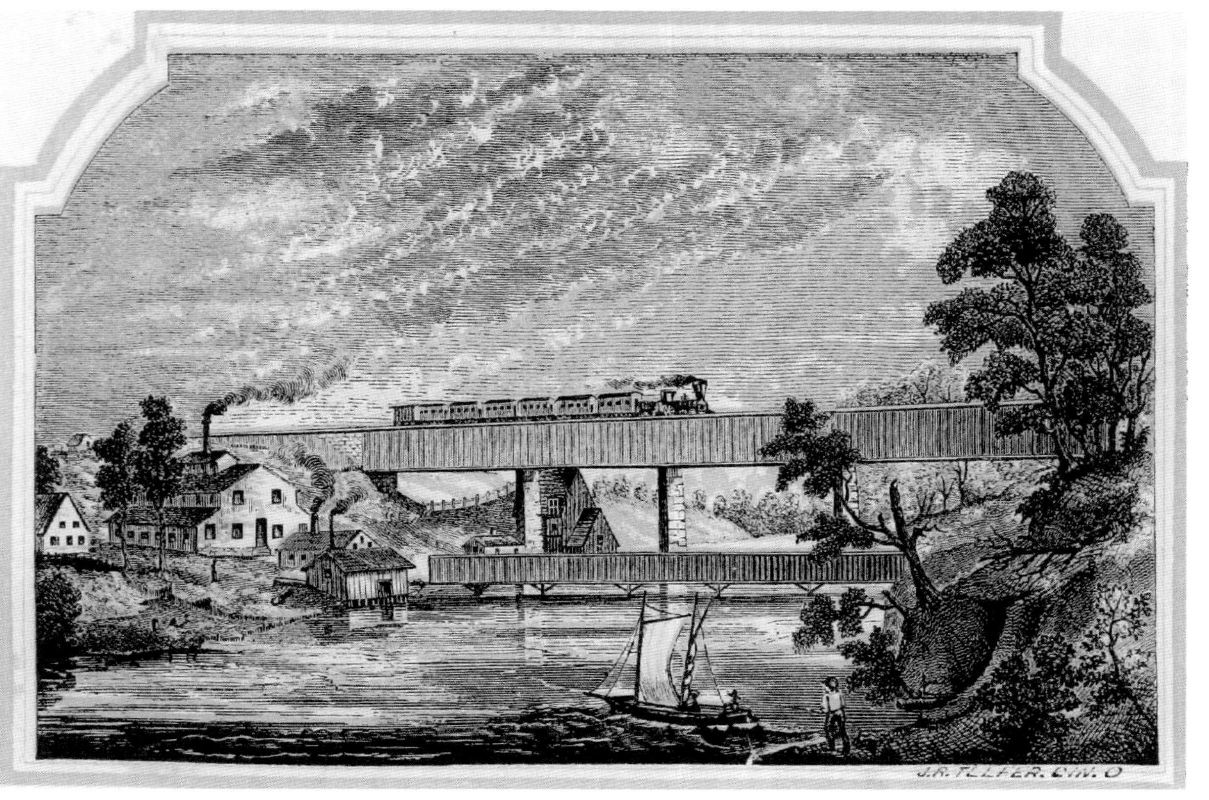

GRAND RIVER, NEAR PAINESVILLE STATION.

country was then full of wild beasts. I have mentioned the bear and the elk; but the most common of the really savage was the wolf. One night, in returning home, Huntington was attacked by a ferocious pack, on which he broke his umbrella to pieces, and only escaped by the fleetness of his horse. The only animal *now* to attack the traveler, is some old ram, who might possibly assault the locomotive, in the simplicity of his ignorance! Sheep have supplanted wolves, and cattle the bears.

We are now three miles from the Lake, and will seldom come in sight of it. At the mouth of Grand River is FAIRPORT, a Lake harbor of considerable importance. It has a number of warehouses and stores. The harbor is an excellent one, and vessels can make Fairport when they can hardly reach any other port.

PERRY STATION is 35 miles from Cleveland.

The Railway is very seldom in sight of the Lake, and generally passes through woods. As we go through this portion of the road, into Ashtabula county, and Pennsylvania, we shall often meet with pine trees, whose straight trunks and deep green contrast strongly with the common forest trees of Ohio. We are approaching now the borders of a very large district, in which the pine predominates. From the shores of Lake Erie, in eastern Ohio, and in Pennsylvania and New York, far into the interior, on the head waters of the Allegheny, the Genesee, the Chemung, and the Susquehanna, the pine tree is everywhere the principal object in the forest. The New York and Erie Railroad passes 200 miles through this pine region, and every year immense quantities of this lumber are shipped from various points on the Allegheny, the Genesee and the Susquehanna. This region has been almost the only source of supply for pine lumber for the upper Ohio. In past years, Cincinnati has been supplied with boards and shingles from the Allegheny. They were floated down in rafts in the spring, when the waters were high. In the month of April, the shores of the Ohio at Cincinnati, have sometimes been lined for miles with rafts of pine lumber. How long the Allegheny and Genesee country may be able to continue this supply, is doubtful. Already a great deal of lumber is brought to Cincinnati by canal, from Michigan; and I have no doubt the time will come when nearly all the pine lumber required for Cincinnati, will be brought from Michigan and Wisconsin by railway. Many persons have doubted whether even coal could be carried by rail; but that doubt is gone —so it soon will be about lumber. Railways are gradually working out a great social revolution; and they will accomplish more than is now dreamed of.

MADISON STATION is 40 miles from Cleveland. We are about 4 miles from the Lake, and 2 miles from Grand River, which for many miles is nearly paral-

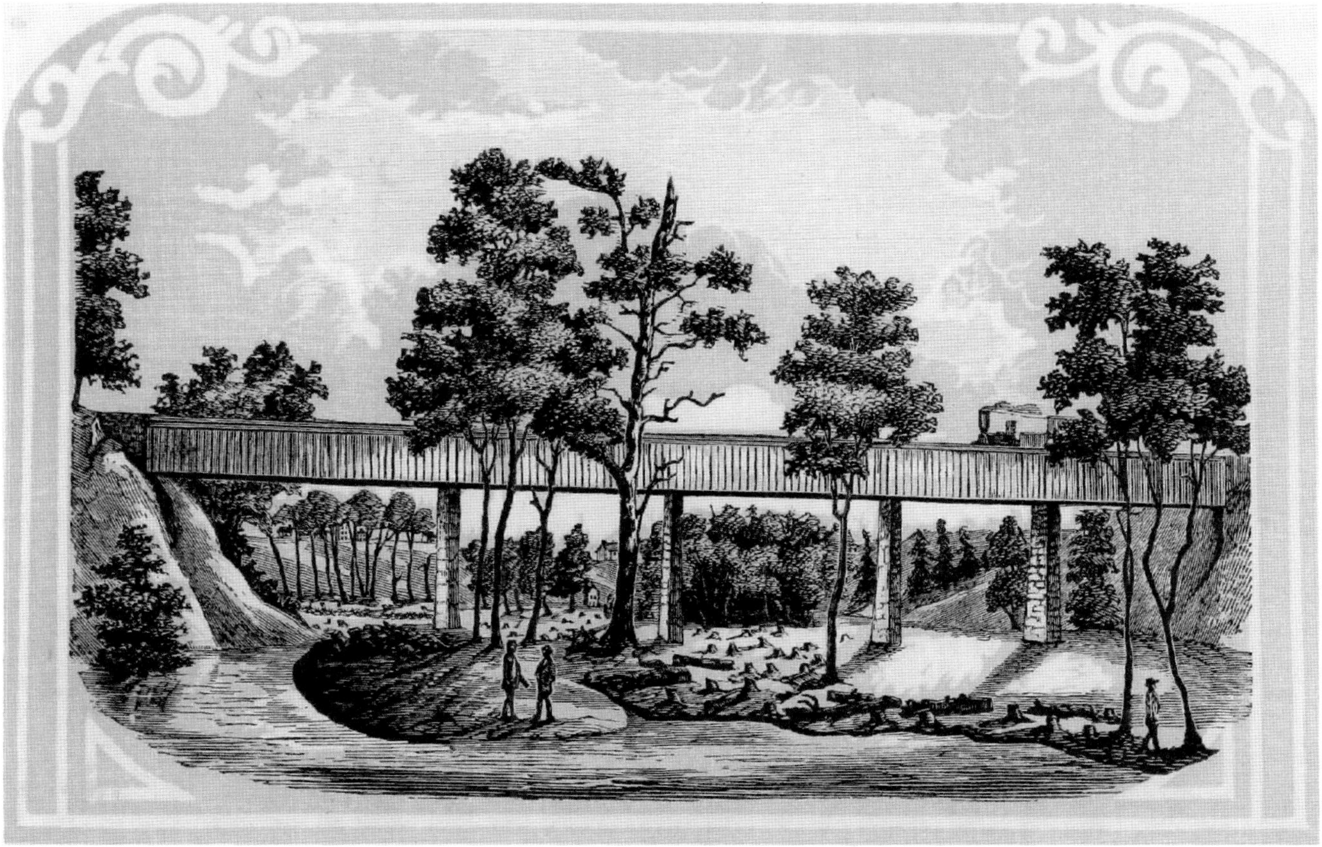

BRIDGE, GRAND RIVER.

lel to the Lake. We are still in Lake county, which is properly named from the Lake, whose shores it hugs for nearly forty miles.

I omitted to mention, that in this county, and several miles south of Painesville, is "LITTLE MOUNTAIN"—one of those natural anomalies, which sometimes occur, to relieve and refresh what might otherwise be a monotonous surface. It is a small, abrupt eminence—about 200 feet in height—from whose summit is a beautiful prospect of the surrounding country, and of Lake Erie in the distance. There is a hotel on the summit—which is a favorite resort in the summer. A cool breeze blows from the Lake, while the earth below is clothed in verdure and beauty. Such a place would make a fine resting spot for a wearied traveler, and be a novelty in the journey of life. How curious it is, that we are all rushing on to get by everything—however desirable or beautiful—as fast as possible, when, by resting a few hours here and there, we might enjoy all the loveliness of Nature, and refresh our wearied spirits, and visit new scenes. Alas! it is the toil, and not the beauty of life, we seek. It is well to make a pleasure of business; but not so well to make a toil of pleasure. Come, let us hasten on. You will not thank me for my sermon, and I will, perhaps, be as little profited myself. We shall rattle on to the end.

UNIONVILLE, 42 miles from Cleveland, is on the

line of Lake and Ashtabula counties. It is a small village, with two churches, and about 500 inhabitants.

ASHTABULA COUNTY—"Old Ashtabula"—is the northeastern county of Ohio—and we here cross the line which separates it from Lake. Its name is derived from that of the river Ashtabula—which signifies in the Indian tongue, *Fish River*.

This county is the first settled on the Reserve, and the earliest in all Northern Ohio. It was on the 4th of July, 1796—just twenty years after the declaration of independence—that the first surveying party of the Western Reserve, landed at the mouth of Conneaut creek. The party numbered fifty-two persons, of whom two were women—Mrs. Stiles, and Mrs. Greene. In the party, was Moses Cleveland, from whom that city was named. They landed like the Pilgrims at Plymouth, on a new and wild shore, and theirs were the life and toils of the pioneers.

It was the 4th of July, and as it was the nation's birthday, as well as the birth of this settlement, they felt like celebrating this double event as best they could; and so, patriotically, though very simply, did they manifest their rejoicing. "Mustering their numbers," says Mr. Barr, "they sat them down on the eastward shore of the stream, now known as Conneaut, and dipping from the Lake the liquor in which they pledged their country—their goblets, some *tin cups* of no rare workmanship—with the ordnance accompaniment of two or three fowling pieces, discharging the required national salute, the first settlers of the Reserve spent their landing day as became the sons of the Pilgrim Fathers—as the advance pioneers of a population that has since made the then wilderness of Northern Ohio to blossom as the rose, and prove the homes of a people—remarkable for integrity, industry, and love of country."

The next day—5th of July—they erected a large log building, which served as a storehouse and dwelling.

GENEVA STATION, 46 miles from Cleveland. We are now winding through the agricultural townships of Ashtabula. This district is as distinguished, and deservedly so, for those products which are derived from pasturage and cattle, as any other in the United States.

We see but little of it from the cars; but we can readily see from the quality of the land, and the character of the woods, that pasture tillage is the proper culture for this region. The peculiar district for butter, cheese, and wool, is that immediately around us; comprising the counties of Ashtabula, Portage, and Trumbull. The quantities of these articles exported are enormous; exceeding all belief, if the statistics be not examined. From the port of Cincinnati, 270 miles southwest, 140,000 boxes of cheese are exported, most of which comes from these counties. At Cleveland, there arrives annually 2,000,000 pounds of butter; 1,000,000 pounds of cheese, and 1,200,000 pounds of wool—a large portion of which comes from this district. Indeed this whole quarter of the State is chiefly devoted to cattle and sheep; and furnishes a large part of the products of those animals exported.

In this pastoral state, the people, although very intelligent, live simple, quiet, sober lives—not led astray by the pleasures and dissipations of the city. Here, if any where, we may expect to find the country maiden described by Gay:

"What happiness the rural maid attends,
In cheerful labor while each day she spends!
She gratefully receives what Heaven has sent,
And rich in poverty, enjoys content.
(Such happiness, and such unblemish'd fame,
Ne'er glad the bosom of the courtly dame):
She never feels the spleen's imagin'd pains,
Nor melancholy stagnates in her veins;
She never loses life in thoughtless ease,
Nor on the velvet couch invites disease;
Her home-spun dress, in simple neatness lies,
And for no glaring equipage she sighs;
No midnight masquerade her beauty wears,
And health, not paint, the fading bloom repairs.
If love's soft passion in her bosom reign,
An equal passion warms her happy swain;

No home-bred jars her quiet state control,
Nor watchful jealousy torments her soul;
With secret joy she sees her little race
Hang on her breast, and her small cottage grace;
The fleecy ball their busy fingers cull,
Or from the spindle draw the lengthening wool:
Then flow her hours with constant peace of mind,
Till age the latest thread of life unwind."

This picture is not a forced or unnatural one. Thousands of our farmers' daughters in these quiet rural districts, are brought up with this simplicity, innocence, and industry. Let us hope that in after times, these scenes and characters may not be despised in the pleasures of fashion and magnificence of wealth.

SAYBROOKE, 50 miles from Cleveland. We are still passing through the "rural districts." Saybrooke is doubtless named from old Saybrook, at the mouth of Connecticut River; and that was named from Lords Say and Brooke—two of the grantees under one of Charles the II's charters. Names are curious things. I could write an interesting chapter on names. There is a whole code of philosophy and morals, and withal, a most singular history connected with names. Some names are plain enough—such as the *Smiths*, who were undoubtedly named from their trade. Then comes a whole series of *colors*—such as Brown, White, Black, Blue, Orange, and all other kinds of color. Then there come *com-*

pounds of these, which are quite curious. There is Mr. Red-ding, Mr. Red-head, Mr. Red-dish, Mr. Red-heifer, Mr. Red-dington, &c. Then there comes the whole list of *sons*—which are probably most numerous. Such as Mr. John-son, Mr. Robert-son, Mr. William-son, Mr. Smith-son, Mr. Brown-son, &c. But there are others, which defy all derivation, and evidently were given in fancy's freak. There is Mr. Pancake, Mr. Pepper, Mr. Wolfe, &c. These gentlemen have reason to speak ill of ancient dignities, and ancestral honors; for they evidently belong to the class who had no grandfathers. They are very worthy people, as I know; but they do not belong to the descendants of the feudal Barons. Well, it is no matter. Names are not much, any how. Of that truth, we have a signal example in the names of our colored brethren—who flourish as Cæsar, Cato, and Pompey What is fame? a breath in other's mouths. Where is Cato? Where is Pompey? Why, just no where. These colored persons are greater than they; for they have something yet vital about them.

But we must hurry on. We have been through *London* to-day, and to-morrow we must go through *Rome, Palmyra, Venice,* and *Utica.* What a revival of the ancients on these green fields of the moderns! But what of it? These towns will grow just as fast and be just as bright and important to this Republic, as if old Palmyra had never fallen into ruins; nor seven-hilled Rome ever declined. It is the youth of the Republic; and Nature, this green Nature, so rich and beautiful, is ever fair. Thus, when Byron had wandered through the ruins of Greece, he exclaimed:

> Still in thy sun, Mendelis' marbles glare;
> Art, glory, freedom fail, but Nature still is fair!

But what is a name? Let us hurry on, and catch up with Time, which has been flying ahead, while we were talking.

ASHTABULA, 55 miles from Cleveland. Well, here we are, on Ashtabula creek. Ashtabula is a neat village, with pleasant aspect. It has several churches, and the usual proportion of stores, and a population of about 1,000.

We are here 2½ miles from Ashtabula Harbor, the mouth of Ashtabula Creek. The Lake steamers generally stop here, and a considerable shipping business is carried on. Several vessels are owned here, and it is one of the principal Lake ports within the district of Cuyahoga.

Ashtabula received a severe shock in the loss of the Washington steamer, which was owned here. She was burned off Silver Creek in June, 1838, and about 40 lives lost. This misfortune has a melancholy interest, from the circumstances attending it. Fire is always a terrible element; but a fire in a vessel at sea—how terrible!

The Washington had left Cleveland in the morning, and a little after midnight, when off Silver Creek, was discovered to be on fire. From a deep sleep the passengers were alarmed by the awful cry of—fire! Then ensued a scene of indescribable confusion and distress; but, while there was a chance of putting out the flames, hope still whispered in their ears. But alas! for its delusion. The fire triumphed; the flames rose high, above all effort to suppress them, and then dark despair seized upon their bewildered minds, and some plunged into the waves, and some seized boards and jumped over, and some remained to be burnt up in the wreck. Then rose the wail of mothers and children, of sisters, husbands, fathers, and was borne over the dark waters.

Ah! few shall part where many meet;
The wave shall be their winding sheet:
And ev'ry billow on the shore
Shall their sad loss in grief deplore.

The small boat saved 25 persons. Other small boats came off, and a few more were saved. But, after making all allowance, it is known that at least 40 perished.

The accidents to steamboats on Lake Erie have been quite severe; but still, so beautiful is the scenery of the Lake, in a clear day, and so cozy and pleasant is that mode of conveyance, that many persons still tempt the hazards of fire and storm.

But here we are, on the Lake Shore Railroad, and whatever else happens to us, we shall not be drowned in the Lake. On the whole, railways are the safest of all modes of conveyance yet discovered, unless we except canal boats—which may the angels save us from! Here we go again; hurry—scurry—fly!

KINGSVILLE—61 miles from Cleveland. The village is a little to the south of the Railroad. It is a pleasant town, with several churches, and 500 inhabitants. It is one of a large class of villages which here, as in New England, may be found scattered over the face of a rural country.

CONNEAUT, 68 miles from Cleveland, is rather an important place, being in the extreme north-east of Ohio, and a considerable Lake port. It is 300 miles from Cincinnati, on a straight line, and 320 miles by Railway, being on one extreme of a diagonal line across the State. It is situated on Conneaut Creek, a stream having a good deal of water power, and on which there are many mills and factories.

Conneaut Borough has several churches, and about 1000 inhabitants. The port of Conneaut has a light-house and several warehouses. It is the entrepot for the landing of supplies and the shipping of produce for a large and fertile agricultural region, not only of the adjacent country in Ohio, but of an important section of Pennsylvania.

On the opposite side is a view of the bridge over Conneaut Creek.

CONNEAUT has been called the "Plymouth of Ohio;" for here, as we have before stated, was the first landing, as we may say, of the pilgrims to the "Western Reserve," in 1796. The spot where Conneaut port is, was then a mere sand beach, overgrown with timber.

The early settlers say the harbors on the Lakes were in those days frequently choked up with sand. The mouths of the streams were continually shifting, until the artificial harbors were built. These improvements have, in a great measure, remedied those evils, and made the mouths of the streams far more healthy.

The first *permanent* settlement of Conneaut was made in 1799. The spot was then inhabited by the Massauga tribe of Indians, who were afterwards obliged to leave, in consequence of the murder of a white man. This spot was likewise the scene of an act of maiden generosity not inferior to that of Pocahontas. Two young men taken in St. Clair's defeat, were brought prisoners to this village. They were obliged to run the gauntlet, and having been kicked and cuffed, it was solemnly decided that one should be saved, but the other should be burned. He was tied to a tree, and hickory bark tied into faggots and piled around him. Just then a young

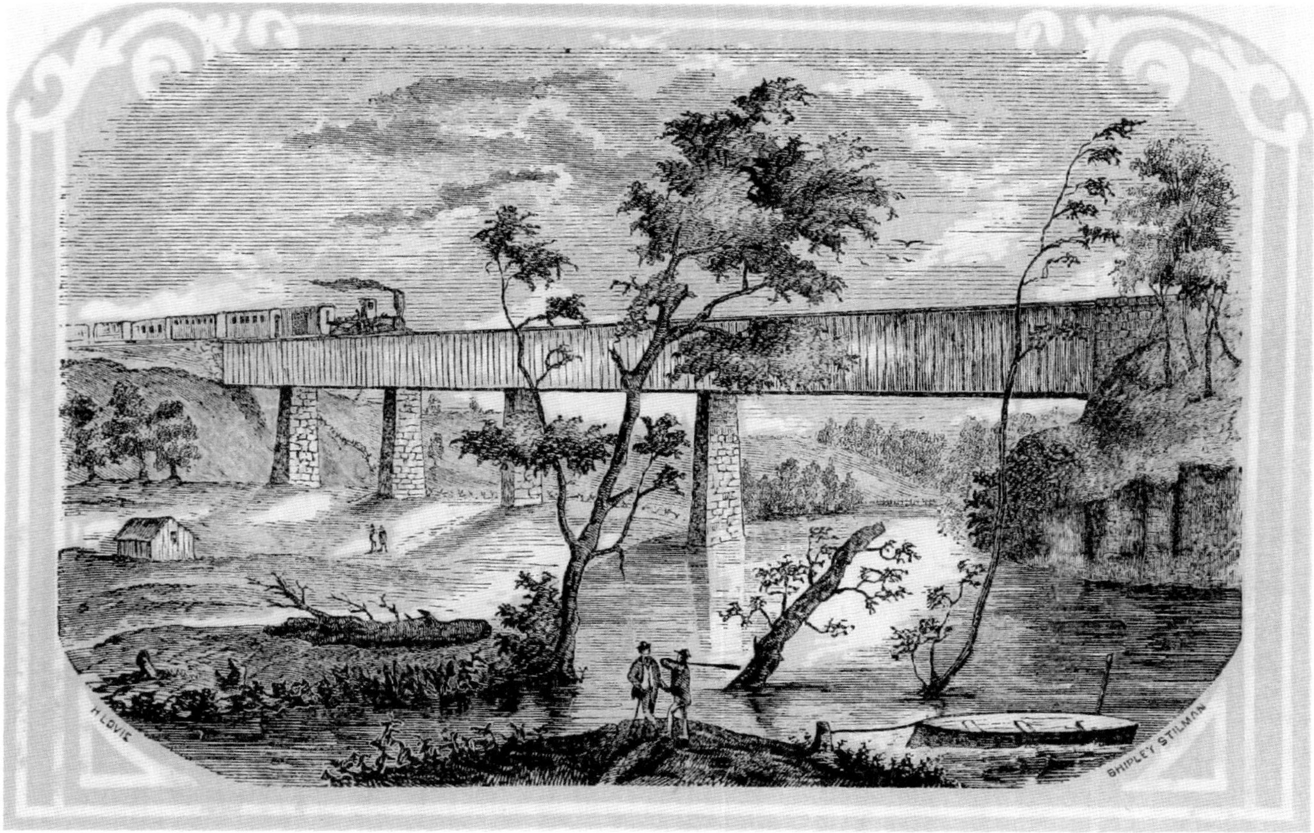

BRIDGE, CONNEAUT RIVER.

squaw, touched with sympathy, sprang forward, and interceded for him. She urgently expostulated, and by the aid of some furs, succeeded in delivering him. We have not her name, but the fame of this lovely maiden should mingle in history with that of the virtuous in every age. The story ends with this heroic deed; and whether there was any episode of romance connected with it, we know not. But we are quite sure our young readers will imagine there was. One thing we are certain of, that the young man must have been without either love or gratitude, if he did not offer his hand and heart, and lay whatever of fortune he might hope for, at the maiden's feet. What if her skin was tanned, and her mind unlearned! her soul was as pure, her life as innocent, as though she had graced the dwellings of the high and honorable.

It was at Conneaut occurred an adventure on the water which has perhaps never been surpassed in perils anywhere. It is told in Howe's Ohio. Mr. Solomon Sweetland had been accustomed, by the aid of a neighbor—Mr. Connies—and a few hounds, to drive deer into the Lake, where, pursuing them with a canoe, he easily shot them. In September, 1817, on a lovely autumn morning, Sweetland rose at dawn, and, without putting on coat or waistcoat, left his cabin, and impatiently waited for the dogs. Soon his ears heard their deep baying; and, arrived at the beach, he perceived a deer had already taken to the water, and was some distance from the shore. He threw his hat on the beach, took to his canoe, and hurried after in animated pursuit. The wind, which was from the south, had increased in the night, and now blew quite strong; but Sweetland forgot the danger in the excitement of the hunt. The deer hoisted his tail in defiance, and stoutly breasting the waves, showed that in a race with a canoe, the event was not certain. When Sweetland overtook him, he first became aware of his situation; for the deer turning, shot past him towards the shore; and he tacking, discovered that he could make no progress towards the shore, but was continually drifted farther to sea! Now came a time of fearful trial to himself and friends. He had been seen by Mr. Connies and his family, from the shore, as he gradually disappeared from sight. In vain did three of his neighbors generously put off in a light boat to his rescue. In vain did they search the raging waters. The deer was seen returning to the shore, but the man was lost from sight. Where was Sweetland? The canoe was a large one, dug out from a fishing boat, and was considered a superior one of its kind. Sweetland continued to head towards the land, in the faint hope that the wind might abate, or aid come to his relief. One or two schooners came in sight, but he signaled them in vain. The shore continued in sight, and on its distant outline, he could trace the spot where stood his cabin and his loved ones; but in vain he struggled to near them. At last these familiar objects receded from his sight, and sunk, and the shores sunk below the troubled waters. He was alone on the stormy deep! His frail canoe alone upheld him, and the spirit of the tempest alone uttered its voice in his ear!

One only chance remained—and as he was a good sailor, with a cool head and stout heart, he seized upon that. This was to put the boat before the wind, and strike for the Canada shore, fifty miles off! It was now blowing a gale, and he was borne towards the shore with fearful power. He was obliged to stand much of the time to steady and guide the boat; and he was obliged sometimes to bale with a pair of *shoes!* Then came the night, and its shadows gathered round him. The sky was overcast, and only here and there a twinkling star sent its ray through the darkness. Destitute of food and clothing, he was thus rocked upon the billows, in that long and dreary night. At morning he saw the shore, and found he had made Long Point, Canada. Here he had an adverse wind and cross sea; but the merciful Providence which had guided him so far, enabled him to land. But his trials were not ended. He was forty miles from any settlement—and the way lay through marshes and thickets. Still, with a stout heart—though weary and faint—he managed to crawl on, till he arrived at the habitations of men. On his way, he found a quantity of goods—the remains of some wreck—which, after he got refreshed and strengthened, he brought off, and thus made an accession to his little fortune. He proceeded to Buffalo, and thence by vessel to Conneaut—where he found his funeral sermon had been preached, and he had the rare privilege of seeing *his own widow* in mourning for him!

Farewell to Ohio! Green buckeye land, we must leave thee for a time. Rich are thy fields, and pleasant thy homes—long shall we remember thee when far away!

PENNSYLVANIA, HAIL! The Pennsylvania line is 70 miles from Cleveland, and here we enter the Keystone State. Pennsylvania is one of the oldest and most interesting of the States. You know that it was settled first by William Penn and his Friends, (as the Quakers always call themselves), at Philadelphia; but then that was long before the settlement of this northwest corner—and it was also a very different kind of immigration. In this part of the State, there was no such quiet and peaceful progress as was made at Philadelphia. On the contrary, it was a scene of trouble and conflict—as Indians, French, English, and Irish, alternately held sway. I say Irish, because after the English prevailed over the French, the principal immigrants to Pittsburgh, and all the surrounding counties, were the Scotch-Irish, or those from the north of Ireland, which, after Cromwell's Conquest, was settled by the Scotch.

The northwestern part of Pennsylvania was first *stationed*—not settled—by the French, who built Fort Du Quesne, at Pittsburgh, a fort at Presque Isle, (now Erie) and others on French creek. At that time, however, the Indians were still the proprietors of all the lands west of the Alleghanies, and the French only held a line of posts on the Ohio, the Lakes and their tributaries. From these posts they were ultimately driven by the English; but it is difficult to tell exactly when the first permanent settlers came to this district.

We are now entering Erie county, through which runs French creek, and on which was the scene of the earliest adventures of George Washington. In 1753, Governor Dinwiddie of Virginia, having discovered that the French were establishing posts on the Ohio, and being unable to obtain accurate information by his messengers, selected a young surveyor, who at the age of nineteen had received the rank of Major, and who was inured to hardships and woodland ways—while his courage, judgment, and firm will, all fitted him for such a mission. This young man was George Washington, then but twenty-one years and eight months old. He left Williamsburg with a Mr. Gist for his guide, and arrived at Wills creek, where Cumberland now is, on the 15th of November, and on the 22d, reached the Monongahela. Thence he went to Logtown, and held long conferences with the chiefs of the Six Nations, living in the neighborhood. Finding the French and Indians above would not come down to meet him, he proceeded to their forts. Traveling in cold and rain, he reached Venango, at the mouth of French creek, on the 4th of November. This was an old Indian town, and here he found the French—who with rum and flattery had very nearly seduced the friendly Indians who went with him from Logtown. Patience and good faith, however, conquered, and after another rough time, through snow, rain, and cold, he reached the fort on French creek. This was only fifteen miles from the present Erie. Here he was politely told by the French commander, that the demand of Governor Dinwiddie to evacuate the forts, could not be complied with. The shrewdness and capacity of Washington, as a military man, was even then quite conspicuous. He took accurate note of the fort, armament, men, provisions, &c., and communicated them to his government. In the same expedition, he also observed the admirable situation of the junction of the Allegheny and the Monongahela—and at his recommendation a fort was built there.

On his return, young Washington suffered severely, and very nearly lost his life. He left his friendly

Indians, and with Gist set out on foot for Wills creek. Accepting the guidance of an Indian, he was betrayed and shot at. In the midst of winter, they came to the Allegheny, expecting to cross on the ice, but were disappointed, and compelled to make a raft with a single hatchet. Nearly frozen, they were thrown upon a desert island. The ice fortunately made that night, hard enough to bear them, and they escaped to the main land. Thus, through hardships and dangers, Washington returned safe to Williamsburg. It was in such a school of bodily, as well as moral and intellectual training, that Providence was gradually fitting Washington to become the Man of the Revolution.

ERIE COUNTY, in which we are, comprehends the whole of that portion of Pennsylvania, bordering on the Lake. The Lake shore of Pennsylvania is about 50 miles—thus giving her, like New York, a territory extending from the Ocean to the Lakes. This is peculiar to these two States, and a great advantage. Erie county contains nearly 40,000 inhabitants—raises a large quantity of grain and potatoes; but deals chiefly in cattle and sheep—pasturage being everywhere the principal element of Lake-shore farming.

SPRINGFIELD STATION is 76 miles from Cleveland. The town is to the south of the railroad. It is a small village, with several stores and mills.

The scenery of the Lake shore varies but little. We pass no high hills, and the varieties of surface are produced almost altogether by the rivers, creeks, and ravines, which terminate in the Lake. The shores of Lake Erie, have, as a residence, however, some great advantages. The land is generally level; the air cool and bracing; the temperature not severe; the scenery, like that of the Ocean, grand and various—at one time like a transparent mirror, reflecting the light sails of the water craft, and shining in the dazzling rays of the sun; at another clothed in the gloomy grandeur of the storm; at another mixed with all the elements of sun and shade, of clouds and sky, of curling waves and of moving vessels.

It was a remark of Volney, the traveler, "that the southern shore of Lake Erie would one day become the pleasantest part of the United States, and lined with the homes of a numerous people." The prediction is, in some degree, accomplished—for we have already such cities and towns, as Buffalo, Cleveland, Erie, Sandusky, Toledo, and other flourishing places; and the intermediate shore is rapidly filling up with intelligent and prosperous citizens.

GIRARD STATION, 80 miles from Cleveland. This is a small post town of Erie county, containing about 400 inhabitants.

FAIRVIEW is a village at the mouth of Walnut creek.

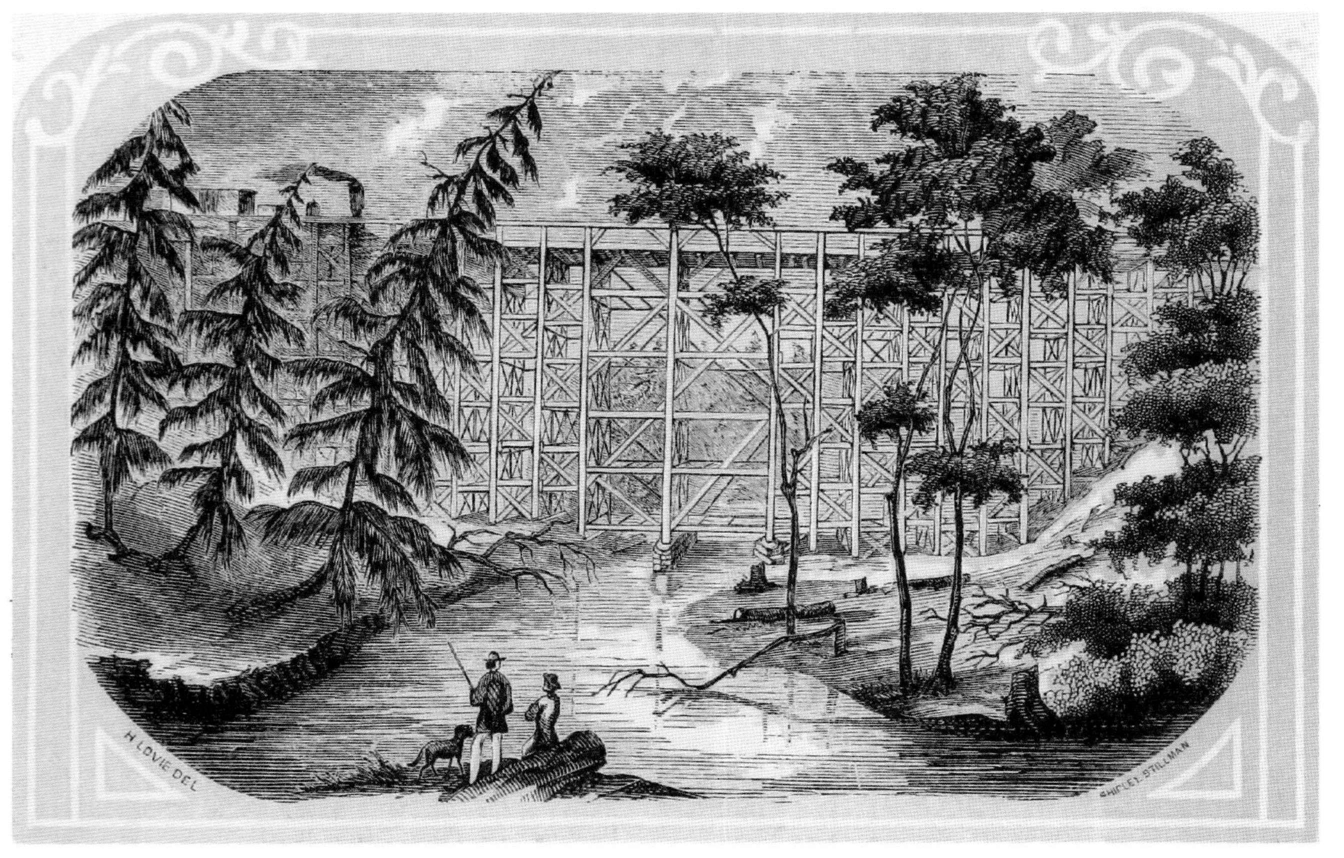

BRIDGE, CROOKED CREEK, NEAR SPRINGFIELD, PA.

What is History? We are here in the very midst of the civilization of the Earth. We are near the city of Erie. In twenty hours we shall be in the great city of New York, which, with its surroundings, has a million of people. We are moving on the newest and greatest element of civilization—the Railway. We are in sight of the most splendid steamers. We are surrounded by ladies and gentlemen. With all this, we cannot trace the history of this spot beyond the life of a single man! We are a nation grown up in a day—and beyond a century or two, all on this continent lies in clouds and shadows. I thought of this in endeavoring to get some idea of the first settlement of this district. But I cannot. Robert Proud, who wrote what he called the history of Pennsylvania, about the year 1776, says, "there were then *eleven* counties in Pennsylvania, (there are now sixty-three) of which, Bedford and Westmoreland were the only ones west of the Alleghenies. Of these, he says they are "frontier counties, in the back parts of the province, next the *Indians:* they were laid out but very lately, and are as yet, but thinly inhabited and little improved—being the most remote from the capital of the province." Just think—the great States in the valley of the Ohio, were then, as the sheriff would say, *non est inventus*—and Western Pennsylvania, now flourishing with half a million of inhabitants, was a mere frontier, where the daring emigrant was just building his cabin among the Indians! But what Indians were here? If we know little of the white settlements, we know less of the Indians.

The Indian settlers here were very much in the same pursuit and character as the whites. It does not seem very clear, that there were any *permanent* residents in this region. The Indians who dwelt here, were the outguards or hunters of the great Iroquois confederacy. On the Susquehannah, Beaver creek, and possibly along the whole Lake shore, the Indian inhabitants were the *Delawares*—a leading tribe of the Iroquois. These did not belong strictly to the Six Nations; but were united with other tribes in another confederacy. The Delawares were among the most renowned, as well as noble families of aboriginals. They seldom exhibited the traits of meanness and ferocity, so common with most Indian tribes; but were generally fair and honorable. The Delawares, like most of the Eastern tribes, have nearly died out. The remnants of the tribe were removed beyond the Mississippi, where they still remain.

ERIE, OR PRESQUE ISLE—95 miles from Cleveland, 348 miles from Cincinnati, and 507 miles from New York, *via* the N. Y. and Erie Railroad.

We are now at a very remarkable place, naturally, historically and socially. We are at one of the great points on the great Lake frontier. I must tell you a little more of it than of most towns. The name was originally PRESQUE ISLE—so called by the French —which signifies *almost an island;* for such is the fact. On the west of the bay, a long peninsula runs nearly parallel with the eastern or southern shore, so as almost to inclose what is now the bay and harbor of Erie. This peninsula has latterly been converted into a real island, by the gradual wearing away of the isthmus, which connected it with the main land, so that the harbor of Erie has now two entrances. It will readily be seen that this geographical conformation makes one of the very best harbors that can be conceived; but for a long time a great difficulty was experienced, as in nearly all the Lake ports, by the formation of a sand-bar across the entrance. The United States government has expended here a great deal of money, in making piers and improvements for the harbor. The water on the bar is now from 8 to 10 feet—quite sufficient for such craft as navigate the Lake.

ERIE lies beautifully, on a bluff on the south side of the bay and peninsula. Erie is the modern name. As I said before, it was called by the French, who were the earliest settlers, Presque Isle. It appears to have happened this way: In 1748, several Virginians, among whom were Thomas Lee and two brothers of George Washington, associated themselves together, as the "Ohio Company," for the settlement of western lands. They obtained an order from the British government on the government of Virginia, for half a million of acres, two hundred thousand of which were to be located at once; which were to be held ten years without rent, on condition that within seven years one hundred families were put upon it, and a fort built for their protection. This the company proposed to do at once. Other companies were formed, and other grants made. But before this, the French had made settlements on the lower Ohio, and on a line between them and Canada. This attempt to settle the upper Ohio, therefore, at once excited their jealousy. They saw that if the English got a foothold here, they would descend and fall on the French posts below.

In February, 1751, Christopher Gist, the same person who went out afterwards with Washington, went out as the agent of the "Ohio Company," to examine the western lands, and was gone seven months, descending as low as the falls of Ohio. In November of the same year, Gist commenced a thorough survey of the lands east of the Kenhawa, which were to be occupied by the Kenhawa Company. In the meanwhile the French were not idle. They took immediate steps to fortify posts on the upper Ohio. They began by establishing a post at this place—Presque Isle, or Erie, on the Lake. From Erie they opened a wagon road to a little lake at the head of French Creek—about fifteen miles—and there they built another fort. These were the first settlements of Erie county, and were made more than a hundred years ago.

Thus, too, began what is called the "Old French War;" and in that began thé military education of George Washington, the leader and hero of our revolution. The French continued to build their forts and posts. The English did the same. The French tampered with the Indians. The English counteracted them; and so mutual aggressions and encroachments were made, till blood was shed and the war commenced. "It was now," says Mr. Perkins in his Annals, "April, 1754. The fort at Venango was finished, and all along the line of French creek, troops were gathering, and the wilderness echoed the strange sounds of a European camp—the watchword, the command, the clang of muskets, the uproar of soldiers, the cry of the sutler; and with these were mingled the shrieks of drunken Indians, won over from their old friendship by rum and soft words. Scouts were abroad, and little groups formed about the tents or huts of the officers, to learn the movements of the British. Canoes were gathering, and cannon were painfully hauled here and there. All was movement and activity among the old forests and on the hill sides, covered already with young wild flowers, from Lake Erie to the Allegheny."

So began, in these wild woods, on the shores of Lake Erie, and on the beautiful Ohio, the first clash —the first alarm—the first battle cry of that great war, which engaged all Europe; which was scarcely interrupted by the peace of 1763, when the murmurs of the Revolution began, and which continued to roll on from revolution to revolution, overturning and overturning, till the battle of Waterloo—sixty years of terrible conflict, resulting in the independence and liberty of America, and the commencement of a great social and political change in all the nations of Europe.

So began the settlement of Erie; but Erie was for half a century, though important as a position, but a small village. In 1763 it was attacked and taken by a confederacy of hostile Indians. In 1794, it was threatened by the celebrated Brant, in consequence of a dispute between the United States and the Six Nations, as to the erection of a fort there.

In writing to the British authorities, Brant says, "In regard to the Presque Isle business, should we not get an answer at the time limited, it is our business to push these fellows hard, and therefore it is my intention to form my camp at Point Appineau; and I would esteem it a favor of his excellency the Lieutenant Governor, to lend me four or five batteaux.

Should it so turn out, and should these fellows not go off, and O'Bail continue of the same opinion, an expedition against these Yankees must of consequence take place."

This was written in July; but the decisive victory of Wayne, in August, over the Indians of the northwest, ended, if there ever existed, any desire of the Six Nations to war about Presque Isle.

Connected with these Indian wars, was another event of great interest: the death of Anthony Wayne —the MAD ANTHONY of the Revolution. Wayne is one of the most remarkable names in American history; and it was *here* the great soldier died. He was on his return from Detroit, in 1796, where the treaty of Greenville had been made, and the British posts evacuated, when he was taken suddenly sick, and died at Erie. There was a good deal of mystery, and some talk about the circumstance of his death. He had a controversy with General Wilkinson, who was then, and indeed always, of rather doubtful standing in the public mind. It was said that Wayne had important papers affecting Wilkinson, in his trunk. However that was, Wayne suddenly died at Erie, and his bones were finally carried to Chester county, Pennsylvania, whence he came.

ANTHONY WAYNE was a remarkable man. He was born in Chester county, Pennsylvania, in 1745. His father was a farmer, of excellent character, who rendered considerable service to the government. He took great pains to educate his son, especially in the sciences. Anthony entered the army, as Colonel, in 1775, accompanied one of the expeditions to Canada, and was shot in the leg at the action of the Three Rivers. In 1776, he was made a Brigadier General. He fought at Brandywine, at Germantown, at Monmouth, and finally stormed Stony Point, on the Hudson, in 1779. It was for this desperate action he received the *soubriquet* of "Mad Anthony." He was in the campaign against Cornwallis, and was finally appointed to the command of the southern army. In fine, there was not an important battle, or hazardous enterprise, from the beginning to the end of the Revolution, in which he was not more or less distinguished. His career was a brilliant and successful one.

When the Revolution was closed, the constitution framed, and the Northwestern Territory constituted, Wayne was called upon a new theatre of action. Hamar and St. Clair had both been defeated by the Indians; the latter most disastrously. In this condition of affairs, our whole northwestern frontier was exposed, the people disheartened, and the Indians triumphant. It was at this time, that Washington, who well knew the character of Wayne, appointed him to the command of the Northwestern army. In the summer of 1792, he was busily engaged in collecting his troops, and in training and disciplining them for the particular service they were meant for. In December, 1792, the army which was called Legion of the United States, assembled at Legionville, twenty-two miles below Pittsburgh. There it passed the winter, till April, 1793—when, being taken down the river, it encamped on the present town plat of Cincinnati, and near Fort Washington. There—in consequence of the negotiations carried on by Commissioners—it remained till October, being engaged in drilling and preparations. On the 7th October, 1793, Wayne and his "Legion" left Cincinnati; but encamped at what is now Greenville, Darke county. In the meanwhile, the field of St. Clair's defeat had been recovered, and "Fort Recovery" built there. In June, 1794, Fort Recovery was attacked by Little Turtle, with 1000 warriors, but after a severe contest, he was repelled. Wayne declared that there were many white men with them, and the Indians were really instigated by the British. On the 8th of August, "Fort Defiance" was built at the junction of the Auglaize and the Maumee. At length, on the 20th of August, Wayne encountered the united forces of the Indians on the Maumee, and completely defeated and overwhelmed them in a decisive battle. This battle was in fact, the close of the Revolution. Up to this time, the British had never delivered up the western posts, in conformity with the Treaty of 1783. On the contrary, it was clearly proved that the British authorities in Canada, had instigated and excited the Indians in their hostilities. The battle of the Maumee, however, ended all this, and soon after the posts in the northwest were delivered. The spirit of Wayne is very well illustrated by a terse and piquant correspondence between Major Campbell—who commanded the British post on the Miami—and Wayne, after the battle of Maumee. Campbell demanded to know why the American Army had taken a post "almost within reach of the guns of a fort occupied by his Majesty's troops;" to which Wayne replied that "were you entitled to answer, the most full and satisfactory one was announced to you from the muzzles of my small arms yesterday morning, in the action against the horde of savages in the vicinity of your post, which terminated gloriously to the American arms; but had it continued until the Indians, &c., were driven under the influence of the post and guns you mention, they would not have much impeded the progress of the victorious army under my command, as no such post was established at the commencement of the present war between the Indians and the United States."

Wayne, after the battle, proceeded to Detroit, there to finish the business of the war, and the posts. Having remained in the northwest more than a year longer, at the close of 1796, he took passage in a sail vessel for Erie, on his way to Washington, to answer some secret charges preferred against him by Wilkinson, but which were known to few, and were never publicly made. When near Presque Isle, (Erie), he was taken (it was said) with gout in the stomach, suddenly died, and was buried on the shores of the Lake. Some years after, his body was taken up and removed to his native place—Chester, Pennsylvania. It was quite singular that when taken up, his body was still fresh and quite preserved. This was probably caused by some peculiar property of the earth or fluid, in which he was buried.

Wayne was about 57 years of age at his death, and, on the whole, was probably the most successful General of the Revolution—and certainly one of the most brilliant, brave, and skillful. The soubriquet of "Mad Anthony" lives embalmed in memory, and fresh with glory.

ERIE CITY—Presque Isle—is now a large, beautiful and flourishing place. I have visited it three times in the last thirty years, and each time it had greatly improved. It lies on the south shore of the Lake, on a bluff situated on and overlooking Presque Isle Bay. The plan of the borough extends three miles along the Lake, by an almost equal depth. The principal street lies from the harbor, on the road to Waterford. It has eight or ten churches, schools, seminaries, banks, mills, factories, stores, and all the machinery and adjuncts of a busy, thriving place. It employs a large capital, and has some 8000 inhabitants.

During the war of 1812–15, this was a rendezvous and naval station for the United States marine on Lake Erie. Here Perry's fleet was built in about *seventy days* from the time the timber was standing in the forest! To this place he returned, after a glorious victory, with his prizes, and his vessels were afterwards sunk in the harbor near the navy yard. The Lawrence, his flag ship, was recently in part out of water, and visitors would frequently cut relics from its hulk.

To the right of the town, on a high bank overlooking the bay, are the remains of the old French fort —Presque Isle—now overgrown with weeds. Half a mile beyond it, is the blockhouse, erected for the protection of the navy yard during the late war. Wayne was, at his own request, buried under the flag staff of the fort; but, as I before said, he was removed by his relatives. Forty years have elapsed since the victory of Perry, and Lake Erie has been no more disturbed by the thunders of battle. PERRY, the victor of Erie, has long gone to his final home, where the grass grows over his head.

How sleep the brave who sink to rest
By all their country's wishes blest!

The LAKE SHORE ROAD, upon which we have traveled, passes in the rear of Erie; so that in fact we get but a distant view of the town, which, as we go east, may be seen on the rising bluff to the left. A very good meal may usually be got at Erie; and if the traveler pleases, he can lie over a few hours, to walk round the town, and then resume his journey

The SUNBURY AND ERIE—now provided with ample means—will terminate here, and make a direct connection between Erie and both Philadelphia and New York. Beyond a doubt, this will greatly add to the prosperity of Erie, as well as add new facilities to the commerce of the northwest.

From this point the Lake Shore Railroad will conduct you to DUNKIRK and BUFFALO, thence to any point in the world you may desire to reach. But here, my fellow traveler, you and I must part. I will stop here, and then wend my way back to Ohio, perhaps to Mississippi—who knows?

READER—whoever thou art—farewell! I have taken pleasure in your company, and, although we have met only by the way side, and may meet no more, yet it is pleasant to have met—to have seen together so much of our broad country—to have enjoyed the whirl of motion—the velocity unknown to our fathers—the consummation of modern art. Three hundred and fifty miles we have traveled together, and all has been green, and fresh, and beautiful, and grand; and all has been done by the light of a single day!

Let us call the PAST and the FUTURE to witness this same country under different aspects. The Past comes cold with the winds of the wilderness—dark with the solemn shadows of the forest; surrounded with Indian warriors, and lonely with civilization or art. Slowly she wanders by—overhung with clouds and darkness! Such is the *past.* The present is rich and beautiful. But here comes the FUTURE, draped in all the rich and gorgeous growth of an hundred years. What glorious city is that, panoplied in such vast magnificence? The Queen of the West sweeps by with her million of inhabitants, her splendid temples; her gorgeous paintings; her towers of science; her pictured gardens; her vast array of innumerable arts! And who is this that seems her sister, sitting on the Lake? Thou, beautiful Cleveland, art risen to high proportions! Gem of the Lakes—mart of commerce, thou lookest out upon the waters, like one who holds sovereignty over the waves! And thou, fair Ohio! spread out in all thy affluence of soil, thy culture and thy energy, thou hast become the Imperial State—the abode of millions, the seat of wealth, the residence of glory!

READER dos't *thou* doubt, when beholding what is and what has been, that such shall be? No, thou art made a prophet by this day's travel. Thou knowest—for thou hast seen it—that here, in this central West, is the seat, and material, and power of an Empire. The course of Nature is onward and upward. Empires will be formed in America, as they were in old Asia; but with far higher arts, far greater power of life and glory. Cities are rising here, before whose consummation of splendor, Babylon would have faded into twilight; and Genius will display its inventions on a greater and nobler scale, than the world has ever known.

READER—whoever thou art—farewell! Where-ever thou goest, may thy dreams be pleasant, and thy soul at peace! We have met, like the little waves on the deep—for a time blended, then scattered—rolling on in the bright sun, and presently breaking on the shore! Then, no drop lost, we shall be mingled in the great Ocean of Eternity From that bourne, no traveler shall ever return!——